MANAGING BEHAVIOR
ON THE JOB

More than 80 Wiley Self-Teaching Guides teach practical skills from math to microcomputers, popular science to personal finance. STGs on business and management skills include:

ACCOUNTING ESSENTIALS, Margolis
*ASSERTIVE SUPERVISION, Burley-Allen
BEYOND STRESS TO EFFECTIVE MANAGEMENT, Gmelch
BUSINESS MATHEMATICS, Locke
BUSINESS STATISTICS, 2nd ed., Koosis
CHOOSING SUCCESS: HUMAN RELATIONSHIPS ON THE JOB, Jongewald
COMMUNICATING BY LETTER, Gilbert
COMMUNICATION FOR PROBLEM-SOLVING, Curtis
CREATIVE COST IMPROVEMENT FOR MANAGERS, Tagliaferri
GMAT: GRADUATE MANAGEMENT ADMISSION TEST, Volkell
*HOW TO READ, UNDERSTAND, AND USE FINANCIAL REPORTS, Ferner
IMPROVING LEADERSHIP EFFECTIVENESS: THE LEADER MATCH CONCEPT, Fiedler
LISTENING: THE FORGOTTEN SKILL, Burley Allen
LSAT: LAW SCHOOL ADMISSION TEST, Volkell
MANAGEMENT ACCOUNTING, Madden
MANAGING BEHAVIOR ON THE JOB, Brown
MANAGING THE INTERVIEW, Olson
MANAGING YOUR OWN MONEY, Zimmerman
MEETINGS THAT MATTER, Hon
PERFORMANCE APPRAISAL: A GUIDE TO GREATER PRODUCTIV-ITY, Olson
QUANTITATIVE MANAGEMENT, Schneider
QUICK LEGAL TERMINOLOGY, Volkell
QUICK MEDICAL TERMINOLOGY, Smith
QUICK TYPING, Grossman
QUICKHAND, Grossman
SKILLS FOR EFFECTIVE COMMUNICATION: A GUIDE TO BUILDING RELATIONSHIPS, Becvar
SPEEDREADING FOR EXECUTIVES AND MANAGERS, Fink
SUCCESSFUL SUPERVISION, Tagliaferri
SUCCESSFUL TIME MANAGEMENT, Ferner
USING GRAPHS AND TABLES, Selby
USING PROGRAMMABLE CALCULATORS FOR BUSINESS, Hohen-stein

Look for these and other Wiley Self-Teaching Guides at your favorite bookstore!

*In preparation

MANAGING BEHAVIOR ON THE JOB

Paul L. Brown, Ph.D.
Professor and Chairman
Department of Psychology
State University College
New Paltz, New York

175 YEARS OF
1807 WJ 1982
PUBLISHING

John Wiley & Sons, Inc
New York • Chichester • Brisbane • Toronto • Singapore

Library of Congress Cataloging in Publication Data:

Author: Brown, Paul L. 1942–
Title: Managing behavior on the job.

  (Wiley self-teaching guides)
  Includes index.
   1. Organizational behavior. I. Title. II. Series.
HD58.7.B76   658.3'001'9   81–23063
ISBN 0–471–86516–8   AACR2

Printed in the United States of America

20 19 18 17 16 15 14 13

To Marlene, Shannon, and Melanie,
and to the memory of
Eugene L. Brown

ABOUT THE AUTHOR

Paul Brown, Ph.D., is chairman and professor of psychology at State University College, New Paltz, New York. Through his consulting firm, Instructional Design Associates, Dr. Brown has provided behavioral research and training programs to such firms as IBM, GTE, 3M, Avon Products, Norwich-Eaton, TWA, and many others. He and his staff have taught the skills outlined in this book to thousands of managers, supervisors, and executives in manufacturing, sales, and customer service settings.

PREFACE

The behavioral approach, which has made such a great contribution to the fields of education, parenting, mental retardation, and mental health, is now coming of age in the business world. However, not everyone welcomes this innovation. Some will resist the suggestions made in this book. Others will rebel against its basic premise. One executive told me that I'd " . . . be able to see the heel marks all the way down the hall . . . " as I attempted to drag businessmen to an understanding of people and human behavior that challenges their basic concept of who they are and why people behave as they do. Happily, this has not been the case.

Over the last eight years I have had an opportunity to work with thousands of managers, supervisors, and executives. The majority of these men and women reacted in one of two ways. Many welcomed the approach as a confirmation of things they felt they had always known about people and how to manage them, and were happy to see a *systematic* use of these principles. Essentially, these people were encouraged to continue doing what they had been doing all along. Others were forced by their training in Management by Consequences to take a long, hard look at their basic management style and procedures. They were at first somewhat uncomfortable with a behaviorally oriented view of people and their actions. This new approach challenged or ran contrary to their beliefs and understandings. However, in time these men and women embraced what they themselves came to believe was a "better way" of managing and influencing others. Many reported that over time their basic view of people changed.

This book is designed to be a practical guide for the working manager and executive. The projects and case histories are based on actual situations I have come across in my workshops and consulting practice. There are worksheets throughout the text which are condensed versions of the full-page worksheets that are provided, for your convenience, in Appendix Three. I think you will be challenged by what you read, but also intrigued and maybe even inspired.

The Industrial Revolution has shown us what man can make out of the material resources of our planet. We have devised ingenious methods of extracting these resources and molding them into products that make life easier and more enjoyable. However, more recently we have begun to see that unless we weigh the costs versus benefits of technological advances, we may create more problems than we solve. Indeed, we may be harming our quality of life by our very attempts to improve it.

Recently, we have begun turning our attention more to the human resources entrusted to us in the world of business. Research is now showing us that if we are not careful we may in fact harm people by the methods we use to manage them. A major question being asked by many responsible business leaders and researchers is: " Are we getting work done in organizations consistent with the growth and development of the human resources in those organizations, or at the expense of the health and happiness of those resources?" You will find that *Managing Behavior on the Job* and the approach called "Management by Consequences," deal with this concern directly. It is an approach that encourages respect for the individual and demonstrates how this can be consistent with high levels of productivity. Although the scientific principles you will learn are as old as man, their systematic application in the world of work is somewhat new. As a famous psychologist, Dr. John B. Watson, once said, "We have yet to see what man can make of man." If that prospect intrigues you, then so will this book.

Paul L. Brown

ACKNOWLEDGMENTS

This book is the result of over eight years of research, workshops, conversations, and interviews with thousands of employees, managers, training directors, supervisors, and executives. My sincere thanks are extended to them for sharing with me the words, actions, and procedures that worked for them on the job. I have done my best to incorporate what I learned into the approach I call " Management by Consequences." Special thanks to Jim Prescott, Duane Williams, Bill Brooks, Hal Manker, Em Lowry, Cathy Bragato, Bill Langenstein, Lane Beamer, Brian McKay, Hank Schwartz, Will Coatney, Bob Hopping, Bill Waddell, Dave Drabo, Larry Deabler, Mac Caruthers, Bob Luparello, Ed Butchko, Geoff Nye, Ted Garelick, Skip Winsauer, Rich Balbone, John Hadokowitz, and Charles Rose.

Lane Beamer and Denny Jacobson read early versions of the manuscript and made helpful suggestions for improvement.

Dr. Karen M. Hess and Dianne Littwin at John Wiley & Sons provided superb editorial advice and feedback on the manuscript, which considerably improved the clarity and usefulness of the text.

The work of Dr. B. F. Skinner has significantly contributed to and influenced this book and my life.

Tom Tighe and Rogers Elliott of Dartmouth College started me thinking about many of the principles of human behavior that are applied in this book. They also taught me how to differentiate fact from fiction.

My wife and colleague, Marlene Casley Brown, managed my behavior during this period. Her encouragement, advice, understanding, and love have made not only this book possible but also my career. Marlene edited and typed several versions of the manuscript and provided me with needed feedback following the many interviews, discussions, workshops, and site visits we conducted with business-people throughout the United States.

This book focuses on the alternatives to punitive action we can take when attempting to influence others. I now realize that my openness to positive, reinforcement-oriented procedures is not shared by all people. I thank my parents, Eugene and Edna Brown, for using reinforcement-oriented procedures when managing my behavior. I believe the model they provided led me to look in the right places and to recognize a good procedure when I saw it. They knew the value of accentuating the positive.

CONTENTS

CHAPTER ONE
OVERVIEW: BEHAVIOR AND CONSEQUENCES

This book is about the words managers say and the procedures managers use to influence the people who work with them. The words and procedures that managers, supervisors, and executives use in their organizations are their "tools." Just as a sculptor uses tools to create a work of art from a rough piece of stone, a leader in any group must use tools to achieve results through individuals and groups. All of the tools a leader uses can be categorized as either words or procedures, because the only way to influence others is by talking or writing to them (using words) or by doing something (using procedures). (Doing something also includes nonverbal behavior, e.g., gestures or body language.) Saying "Nice work!" to someone, being present at (or absent from) a meeting, a smile, a frown—each is an example of words and procedures that can influence others.

When we observe effective leaders working with people, we learn the words and procedures that work well. In contrast, observing ineffectual leaders who frequently fail in their attempts to influence others helps us to identify which words and procedures do not work or which make matters even worse.

Interviews with employees can also provide insights into the words and procedures used by their supervisors. Most nonmanagement personnel in organizations honestly want to do a good job; they want to be productive and achieve high standards of quality. They also know their supervisor can be crucial to whether they succeed or fail to achieve their employment goals. As a result, they are an abundant source of information about effective and ineffective supervisory and managerial procedures and techniques.

What words or procedures would you use to cope with such problems as:

- Late reports or reports of poor quality
- High error and scrap rates in assembly or manufacturing environments
- Poor quality documentation, lack of teamwork, and slow turnaround time in experiments in a development laboratory

- Absenteeism, lateness, long unauthorized work breaks
- Excessive rework and repair
- A long-term employee who seems to be turned off to the job, never smiles, and always complains about the company and the performance of others
- A person who resists every organizational and procedural change that is proposed and gives you fifteen reasons why it won't work or tells you how they tried that years ago and no one liked it
- A person above you in your organization who puts off making decisions and is slow in allocating resources you need to do your job
- A team member who cannot provide information clearly or succinctly; for example, whenever you ask what time it is, you are told how to build a watch
- A fellow employee, manager, or executive who constantly interrupts others at meetings, makes wisecracks, is sarcastic, and speaks in a loud, offensive manner, with the result that good ideas are sometimes lost and organizational performance suffers
- Systems and people that just don't seem to work any more

The words and procedures you use as a manager are crucial to the success or failure you experience in trying to solve problems similar to these within your organization.

Over the past nine years I have worked with thousands of supervisors, managers, and executives in a wide variety of businesses and organizations and have had the opportunity to observe the words and procedures used by managers in organizations employing fewer than fifty people, as well as those used by managers of large multinational corporations with several hundred thousand employees. By interviewing and observing employees of service organizations, retail businesses, energy and transportation companies, manufacturing and pharmaceutical firms, high-technology research laboratories, and corporations in the information processing industry, I have tried to document why it is that some leaders consistently outperform others.

Management by Consequences (MBC) is the term I employ to describe the set of words and procedures that effective supervisors and managers use in influencing others.* "Effective" means achieving end

*The terms *supervisor*, *manager*, and *leader* all refer to people who influence others. In some companies the individual is called a manager or *first-line manager*. Some companies refer to people who supervise supervisors as managers, whereas other companies refer to such individuals as a *shift supervisor* or *second-line supervisor*. The procedures described in this book can be especially useful at the first and second levels of supervision and management. The reader should note that the terms supervisor, manager, and leader are used interchangeably in this text.

results that serve the needs of the business. A manager can achieve results by beating people down, by yelling a little louder, or by using fear, obfuscation, intimidation, and threats. These techniques will sometimes get the job done, but at the *cost* of human resources—the people—in an organization. Management by Consequences describes an approach used by effective managers to achieve end results, not at the cost of people, but rather by using methods consistent with their growth and development in an organization. Management by Consequences is good people-management.

Many leaders did not read a book, take a course, or participate in a workshop on good people-management to become effective, but they did learn what worked and didn't work by experience, by trial and error. Whether they know it or not, effective people-managers are applying laws of human behavior that work. Management by Consequences is based on the direct observation of what works and why in terms of the natural laws of human behavior. Management by Consequences can help supervisors and managers avoid some of the pitfalls of learning by trial and error by allowing them to benefit from the experience of others. It can also help the employees they supervise, who are often the unwitting subjects of those trial-and-error "experiments."

Effective managers are good at asking two specific questions and using the answers to be better managers. These questions are:

1. Why do people behave the way they do?
2. How can I use the answer to question 1 to enhance my own effectiveness in my organization?

Management by Consequences represents a simple set of principles and procedures that can help provide answers to these two questions. The case history given in the next section illustrates how this may be accomplished.

Using Consequences to Understand and Influence Behavior

Most human behavior can be understood by analyzing its consequences or payoffs. For example, a programmer on a computer software development project seemed to be constantly complaining to his manager. He complained about working conditions, the company pension plan, the poor quality work of other employees, the weather, the cost of gasoline, and a host of other issues. The manager was asked to consider the most immediate consequence for this complaining behavior. It turned out that each time the employee complained, the manager would hasten to reassure him that he was pleased with his work and then try to convince him that he shouldn't let other concerns affect his performance. A typical response from the manager following a complaint from this employee would be: "Look, don't worry about the other programmers— that's my job. You're doing fine work. Just keep up your end; I'll see what I can do about the others." Or, "There's really not much I can do about the changes that division headquarters makes in our programs. You did all you could. I know the quality of what you do. Just keep it up."

The manager felt that the programmer deserved a sympathetic ear and needed some support and encouragement. But the manager also came to realize that the support and encouragement he felt was so important to this employee's well-being was being provided as a consequence for the employee's complaining behavior. The thought occurred to the manager that perhaps his reassurances were making the problem worse.

How could the manager find out whether his reassurances were indeed part of the problem? It was suggested that the next time the employee complained the manager should listen, but not attempt to provide comfort or reassurance. "Changing the consequence might change the behavior." Instead, the programmer was invited to document business-related complaints. At other times the manager would suggest that the employee himself should try to solve a problem. And sometimes the manager would ask the employee if he could put in writing some specific, positive recommendations for improvement that the manager could use to resolve an issue.

Over a two-month period the manager reported a significant decrease in complaints from this employee, and perhaps more importantly, all complaints brought to his attention were business related and accompanied by constructive suggestions for improvement. Although he continued to provide reassurance and encouragement to the employee, those reassurances were now given following good work performance or when the employee raised appropriate issues of concern.

This case history focuses attention on the powerful influence that consequences have on human behavior. Managers, supervisors, and executives provide consequences for the behavior of others throughout the work day. Understanding the true impact and proper use of this influence is what Management by Consequences is all about.

Here is another example of Management by Consequences at work: A participant in a workshop on Management by Consequences explained that he was new to his managerial position and felt very uncomfortable trying to evaluate the performance of his employees, who worked in an automated warehouse. He discussed this with an engineer who was quite familiar with operations of this type. In the engineer's opinion, there were "no positive ways to gauge properly" the employee performance. After some discussion, however, they settled on something they thought they could measure—the number of requisitions filled daily. But because this was an automated storage-and-retrieval system driven by a computer, it was felt that the total number of requisitions filled was determined by the "system," not the individual employees who entered the requisitions into the computer and physically handled cartons and crates. Therefore, the number of requisitions filled seemed to be a measure of the computer's performance rather than a measure of employee performance, and the manager was not sure this number would be a fair standard for evaluating employees.

Nevertheless the number of requisitions filled was tracked for several days. The results showed an average of ten requisitions filled per hour, with some employees filling as many as fifteen and some as few as five. This variance existed in spite of the fact that all employees handled the same material. With that information in hand, the manager called a departmental meeting, and both staff and manager mutually established a goal of fifteen requisitions per hour. All involved felt such a goal was reasonable. The only concern expressed by the employees was that a contingency be built into the system to take into account mechanical failures. The manager assured everyone that this had been done. He also informed them that he was using a 7.2-hour day rather than an 8.0-hour day in calculating daily goals. A new system of posting the total number of requisitions filled by the entire team was also established to provide feedback. Thus, this feedback became a new consequence for filling requisitions. The illustration on page 6 outlines the results of the project.

Prior to the meeting, the department as a group had been averaging 420 requisitions per day. On the day following the meeting, 520 requisitions were recorded; within a week the number had risen to over 600, and by the middle of the second week a rate of 648 requisitions filled daily was attained. At that time the manager asked his upper-level manager to speak to department members, to compliment them on their effort and improvement, and to single out the highest performer for special attention. This recognition from upper management was yet another new consequence for good performance.

In the manager's opinion several benefits resulted from the meeting he held: (1) specific productivity goals were jointly established; (2) friendly competition was stimulated among department members and the rate of requisition filling continued to increase, finally peaking at twenty per hour; and (3) the employees felt that management was finally recognizing the good performers.

One concern raised as the requisition-filling rate continued to increase related to the quality of work. However, it turned out that quality, as measured by number of errors in filling requisitions, actually improved slightly. The manager reported this as a "pleasant surprise."

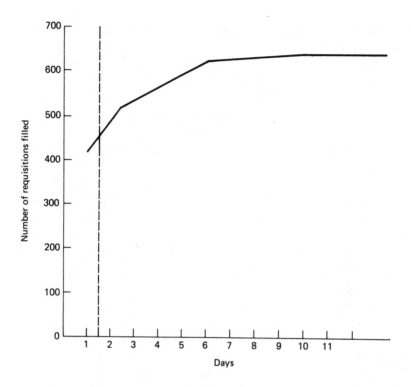

Number of Requisitions Filled by Warehouse Employees

The manager's report of his project stated:

Department morale seems to be very high. There is continuous praise for the department and the people. The employees take real pride in their accomplishments. Many have been promoted. All accomplishments were achieved without additional tools or cost to the company. Everything was there that was needed. It was just a matter of capitalizing on the best resources—people.

Supervisors, managers, and executives will always influence the people they supervise. The proper use of consequences, such as feedback and recognition, is central to the Management by Consequences approach. However, at times more is needed than feedback and recognition. Other procedures, including powerful ones designed to reduce inappropriate behavior directly, are also part of this approach.

Supervisors and managers are paid to influence the behavior and performance of others. One problem many managers run into is the question of control and influence in organizations. Some are uncomfortable with the role of power and influence they are required to play. They deny that they want to have to change other people's behavior. They are wary of any technology of behavior influence and prefer to see themselves as conduits for organizational information and facilitators of work-flow.

I respect this view and find it far more pleasant than the view held by some at the other end of the management philosophy continuum. These individuals are absolutely delighted to be in the position of wielding power over the lives of others. "Build" a better management "two by four" and they will happily use it to get work done through others. These managers know very well that they control the behavior of others in the organization, and in fact wish only that they had more power and control. Far too often such individuals may be found using threats, abusive language, and other coercive, aversive procedures.

Unfortunately, both types of manager can harm and destroy an organization's human resources, the first group by failing to realize just how much influence they do have, and the second by misusing their power. Either shortcoming can be disastrous to organizations and the people who work in them.

Management by Consequences focuses directly on the question of influence, power, and control in organizations. In one sense (though I, too, respond to the harsh connotation of the phrase), supervisors and managers are professional "behavior-modifiers." As is the case with parents and teachers, a manager's success is measured by what is accomplished through others. A manager's day is filled with such tasks as giving instructions, monitoring performance, and providing feedback on performance—all actions that are designed to influence the behavior of others.

Managers modify or influence their employees' behavior everyday; for example, by setting new daily work schedules, moving a manual task onto a computer terminal, or transferring 200 families from one city to another. Managers and organizations must influence the behavior and performance of employees to serve the needs of the business. The question is not whether a manager *will* influence employees; the real question is *how*. How will behavior changes be accomplished? Will they be accomplished in a manner consistent with the growth and development of human resources in the organization, or will behavior changes be accomplished at the cost of these precious resources?

An Influence Model

Management by Consequences is also an influence model. When one person successfully influences another, you usually know it by the end results achieved. A new procedure is adopted, lateness and absenteeism drop, errors decrease, the scrap rate goes down, people smile more often, and opinion survey results improve. When influence occurs, one often sees the results, but not how the results were achieved. MBC is a description of how successful leaders actually influence others.

Just as you may learn to improve your technique in tennis, golf, or skiing by watching slow-motion films or videotapes of experts, you can learn about successful influence by slowing down and "freeze-framing" some of the steps taken by effective influencers of others. MBC contains a set of procedures to help you do this. This approach is based on direct observation of how people influence one another and on sound, proven principles of human behavior. It is a translation of these principles into simple, straightforward, concrete steps that any supervisor or manager can apply to be more effective. MBC is based on the scientific study of why people behave as they do, one of the most humanistic approaches compared to many other styles of management. It focuses on the individual in the organization and epitomizes respect for that individual. This approach helps organizations create environments in which good performance can flourish. It deals with true causes of behavior, not just superficial symptoms, and it helps managers understand the crucial role they play in influencing human behavior and performance.

Operant Conditioning: The Study of How Consequences Affect Behavior

The psychological study of how the environment affects behavior has resulted in some important insights into why people behave as they do. The term *operant conditioning* is used to describe some of these insights.

Operant conditioning is learning that is affected by the consequences of a behavior; hence, the term Management by Consequences. For example, the consequence for the programmer's complaining behavior was receiving reassurance and encouragement from his manager. That reassurance affected the programmer's future behavior. In fact, the result was that the more reassurance given by the manager, the more complaints the employee made. Understanding how consequences affect performance helps us to understand people.

The MBC approach is also useful in analyzing the behavior of persons in supervisory positions. When an office manager asks clerical workers to clean up around their work areas, the request may be followed by a number of possible consequences. One consequence might be that the workers swiftly comply and spruce up the work area. Another possible consequence might be that the workers complain loudly and protest that they don't have enough time, or perhaps tell her "If we stop to clean up, we'll never get out all of today's requisitions." The employees may also take this opportunity to launch into a salvo of other complaints about working conditions, company policy in general, and the office manager's method of dealing with them in particular.

The question now is how will the office manager's future behavior of asking the workers to clean up around their work area be affected by each of these consequences? Faced with such situations in real life, many supervisors report that they continue to ask that the area be cleaned up if the workers comply, but have actually stopped making the request when workers resist and complain.

What does this tell us about the behavior of office managers? Simply that office managers' behavior toward the employees under their supervision is *learned*. That is, the behavior of supervisors changes as a result of the consequences of their behavior. Because different workers provide different behavioral consequences for their supervisors, supervisors behave differently toward them.

How Consequences Affect Behavior

The same behavioral principles hold true for all levels of supervision: Operant conditioning affects the behavior of people regardless of position in the organizational hierarchy. MBC and the principles of operant conditioning stress the importance of two types of consequences:

1. *Reinforcing consequences*, or *reinforcers*, strengthen or encourage the behavior they follow.
2. *Punishing consequences*, or *punishers*, weaken or discourage the behavior they follow.

MBC is not just a fancy title for the old "carrot-and-stick" approach. It is a complete process for understanding our own behavior and that of others. Although it takes into account reinforcing and punishing consequences, it goes far beyond them. As a matter of fact, if the concept of reward and punishment is so simple and basic, why is it that we so often see poorly run organizations and ineffective managers? (And many employees want to know why their boss seems to know only about the "stick"!) The difficulty here is that "rewards" are usually considered a tool that strengthens good performance. Frequently, however, organizations and managers inadvertently reward poor performance and punish good performance.

How Poor Performance Is Reinforced

In the case of the clerical workers complying with the office manager's request to clean up their work area, the manager was *reinforced* for asking them to clean up. In the second case, when workers argued and complained, the manager eventually stopped asking them to clean up. She was *punished* for asking because the consequence of complaining provided by the employees decreased the number of requests she made. This is not, of course, what top management likes to see happen, but in this case this is what occurred.

In the situation concerning the complaining programmer, the reassurances of the manager were actually reinforcing the programmer's complaining behavior. When the manager withheld the reinforcing consequence, the complaining decreased.

In one large printing firm the typesetters reported that the most dependable, hardest-working employees kept getting the toughest, high-pressure jobs, whereas the lazy, complaining workers got the easy, less demanding assignments. It might well be that the supervisors in this firm had learned through experience to assign the tough jobs to the more dependable workers, who in turn reinforced the supervisors for this behavior by getting the job done. On the other hand, the supervisors simply stopped going to the lazy, complaining workers, this response also being a result of the consequences the supervisors received. Destructive, counterproductive "loops" of mutual influence can occur in organizations if managers and supervisors keep giving the toughest jobs to the good employees. When this happens, supervisors have inadvertently punished the good workers for their good performance. As a result, these good employees may get so discouraged and resentful that they stop performing well. However, MBC will show you how to identify such loops and offer ways to avoid them.

We all influence each other all the time. MBC is not a surreptitious technology to be used "on" someone to "fix" them or to squeeze more work out of them. It is an approach designed to help us understand how people *mutually* influence one another. It uses this understanding to improve productivity, the work environment, and the quality of worklife in organizations.

More Than Consequences

MBC does not focus simply on consequences. When we consider how work gets done through people in organizations, two major forces influence behavior: antecedents and consequences. The illustration on the opposite page shows that both antecedents (things that precede or go before behavior) and consequences (things that follow behavior) are used by organizations to get work done.

Effective managers and successful organizations do not simply allow behavior to occur randomly. They use antecedents, such as verbal re-

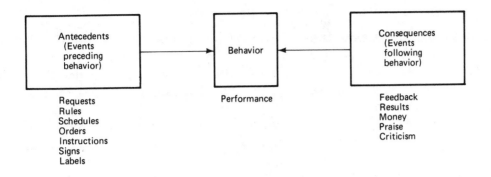

Antecedents (Events preceding behavior)	Behavior	Consequences (Events following behavior)
Requests Rules Schedules Orders Instructions Signs Labels	Performance	Feedback Results Money Praise Criticism

The Major Forces that Influence Behavior

quests, rules, schedules, orders, and instructions, to ensure that the desired behavior will occur and also when it will occur. However, if using antecedents alone is the only thing you do to ensure good performance, you may be doing less than you could to be effective. The figure shows that consequences also have a powerful influence on performance. Both the quantity and quality of performance depend on the nature of the consequences occurring in and provided by an organization. Skillful managers know that properly understanding and using both antecedents and consequences will help to achieve the highest levels of productivity in an organization. MBC is a process that helps you analyze your current use of antecedents and consequences and the impact these procedures have on employee performance. In using the MBC approach you will be able to troubleshoot, change, and fine-tune your personal and organizational practices to create an environment where good performance can flourish.

Just as Management by Objectives (MBO) can show you where you want to go, Management by Consequences provides one very powerful way of getting there. MBC used properly translates into a set of practical, concrete procedures that focus on developing the most valuable resource in an organization—the human resource—to get the work done.

MBC and Productivity

Although productivity means different things to different people, undoubtedly the hourly output of goods and services per worker in the United States has been declining.

Economists have proposed many theories to explain this decline. Among the most frequently proposed are: a slowdown in business investment, a decrease in research and development spending, increased and costly government regulation, higher energy prices, diminishing returns from technological advances, and inflation and "inflation psychology." But none of these experts seems able to provide much of a solution.

Although many grandiose hypotheses may be considered to explain productivity declines, one hypothesis certainly deserves consideration: Perhaps hundreds of thousands of employees are doing slightly less each hour of every working day. It would take only a small portion of the work force to cause such a decline. And while some focus on macrotheories and macrocauses, the Management by Consequences approach focuses on the individual employee—exactly what and how much work each employee is doing each hour of the workday.

The proper use of the basic science of human behavior, which is the core of MBC, has led to literally hundreds of examples of productivity improvement. For example,

- A supervisor in a manufacturing firm increased yield and quality.
- A first-line manager in a financial department helped an employee to improve the quality of presentations to upper management.
- An office manager reduced absenteeism and lateness.
- A marketing manager increased the number of "cold calls" his marketing representatives made, and new accounts increased.
- A middle manager supervising staff professionals at a large company's corporate headquarters increased the number of completed staff reports turned in on time.
- An electrical engineer, who supervised a development project, reduced turnaround time on experiments and increased the number of intermediate deadlines met, resulting in completion of the project on schedule.
- A team of process engineers installed a "people-management" system that resulted in improved yields, shorter process times, and lower "foreign material" counts in a computer chip manufacturing process.
- The vice-president of a trucking firm, using a reinforcement-oriented approach, reduced the average time it took his employees to punch out after parking their trucks, producing a projected annual savings of over $16,000.

Appendix Two contains a list of articles, books, and reports documenting the productivity improvements that have resulted from systematically applying the principles on which MBC is based.

As you progress through this book you will learn how to design your own project to improve productivity or quality in your work setting. (You may want to try your hand at a project at home as well.)

Practical application is the best test of any theory or approach. For years managers and executives have been bombarded with "behavioral science" models that give advice on how to get work done through people. But even though such models provide some good ideas, the most important question is, do they work? How can you test a particular approach? How do you know if and when you're using it? How can you know when someone else is using it? From McGregor's Theory X-Theory Y, through Maslow's hierarchy of needs, up to Herzberg's hygiene theory, and including Mouton and Blake's grid, managers learn about theories that seem to make sense but often leave much to be desired when they try to apply them at work.

You will find MBC refreshingly different. The steps outlined in the remaining chapters will help you develop an action plan for solving a problem of concern to you. MBC is an accountable system with built-in controls that let you know whether it is working. As you learn about MBC you will also find suggested activities and exercises in each chapter to give you practice in the skills involved in each step.

SELF-TEACHING EXERCISE

Self-Quiz

1. How do supervisors and managers influence others?

2. What does the term Management by Consequences (MBC) refer to?

3. Describe an effective supervisor.

4. How do many leaders become effective?

5. What two questions are effective managers good at answering?

6. What two types of consequences affect behavior? Define them.

7. What are the two main forces that influence behavior? Define each one and give examples.

8. What is the relationship of Management by Consequences to Management by Objectives (MBO)?

Answers to Self-Quiz

1. Supervisors and managers influence others with the words they say and the procedures they use.
2. Management by Consequences is a term used to describe the set of words and procedures that effective supervisors and managers use in influencing others. MBC is good people-management.
3. An effective supervisor achieves end results that serve the needs of the business. These end results are achieved in ways that are consistent with the growth and development of people.
4. They learn by trial and error.

5. a. Why do people behave the way they do?
   b. How can I use the answer to question 1 to enhance my own effectiveness?
6. Reinforcing consequences strengthen or encourage the behavior they follow. Punishing consequences weaken or discourage the behavior they follow.
7. Antecedents are events that precede behavior (e.g., requests, rules, schedules, orders, instructions, signs, labels). Consequences are events that follow behavior (e.g., feedback, results, money, praise, criticism).
8. Just as Management by Objectives can show you where you want to go, Management by Consequences provides a means of getting there.

CHAPTER TWO
MANAGEMENT BY CONSEQUENCES: THE FIVE STEPS

The MBC Steps

Management by Consequences is a five-step approach that anyone can use to improve organizational effectiveness. The figure on page 16 illustrates the five MBC steps. Each step translates into a procedural skill that an individual manager can use; however, they are not always followed in lockstep fashion. They might best be considered as elements of a system that may at times be used separately. Managers in such areas as manufacturing, sales, and direct hands-on work will at first find some parts of the approach, such as pinpointing and tracking, easier to apply than managers in highly complex technical areas involving research and development. However, the basic steps and principles apply at *all* levels and in *all* areas of organizations, as examples and case histories throughout this book demonstrate.

An Example

As an overview of the MBC approach, consider the case history describing how one manager in a development lab of a high technology company put them to use. The manager was a participant in a workshop on the use of MBC procedures. Early in the session, participants were asked to pick a problem of concern to them in their departments. One manager—we'll call him Jim—began by saying that the employees in his department were "essentially lazy," had "a bad attitude," and were "unmotivated." Jim's department consisted of two shifts of draftsmen and designers who prepared drawings and other documents for use in manufacturing processes. In effect, his group provided a service to other user groups or in-house "customers."

The first thing Jim was asked following his rather discouraging

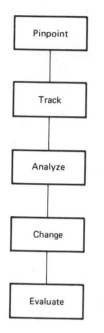

The Five-Step
MBC Approach

statement was how he knew his employees were lazy, had a bad attitude, and were unmotivated. He answered, "Well, I know because they make a lot of mistakes and have about a 55 percent rework rate on design drawings." Without being aware of it, Jim had just put into practice the first two steps of the MBC approach:

1. He had *pinpointed* the problem of "making mistakes."
2. He had *tracked* the pinpointed problem using the 55 percent rework rate as a measure of where things were at the present time. He had already determined a *baseline* measure.

When Jim was asked why he thought the designers were making so many errors, he replied, "Because they're lazy, unmotivated, and have a bad attitude."

It may not sound as if much progress had been made, but now at least Jim had moved toward greater specificity through pinpointing, and he also had an objective measure of the problem through tracking. However, Jim was assuming that he already knew why his employees were performing poorly—because of their laziness, bad attitude, and so on.

Through the workshop Jim learned the use of some basic analytical tools and was encouraged to analyze the effect that current antecedents and consequences were having on his employees' performance. After *analyzing* the environment, he realized two significant things about his management practices:

- *After* an individual employee was identified as making many mistakes, Jim held a one-on-one counseling session to bring the problem to the employee's attention.
- *After* department-wide errors increased to a certain level (as measured by complaints from user groups), Jim held a meeting to discuss errors, mistakes, sloppiness, and rework.

Jim reported that the one-on-one sessions produced some temporary improvement, but that the problem was cyclical: After a few weeks or months the rework rate would begin to rise again and once more Jim had to hold individual and group meetings.

Jim realized that he was providing many consequences for poor performance, but no systematic consequences for good performance. Yet there was good performance! When using a group measure, some employees made almost no errors at least 45 percent of the time. Jim had reported earlier that he knew he had some good people: "Thank heavens for them, but it's the problem employees I find myself spending all my time with."

Jim eventually saw that:

- His current management practices were not working very well.
- His assumption that several of his people were lazy and unmotivated was just that—an assumption.
- His current set of consequences was at best weak and at worst working in the wrong direction.
- He was not systematically providing consequences for good performance.

Based on this analysis, Jim made some very specific changes in his management practices and style. The first one he made was predicted to reduce the company to bankruptcy within 30 days! This innovation was to have employees correct their own errors. The general response was:

"We can't do that; there's no time!"

"This is a high-pressure, quick turnaround job. We just can't wait for people to correct their own mistakes!"

Jim agreed that there probably wasn't enough time for employees to correct their own errors under the current system. However, the present system also had a 55 percent rework problem because the first available employee had been making the corrections; thus, first-shift employees frequently corrected second-shift errors, and vice versa. Such a procedure often resulted in animosity between individuals and shifts, with each shift feeling its members were carrying the company while the other shift was dragging it down.

Jim was determined to try the new procedure because his analysis of the current situation, along with his new knowledge of MBC, impressed him with the need for improved feedback systems. If employees did not know of their mistakes, how could they be expected to improve? Seeing their own errors might help. In addition, because most errors appeared to result from carelessness, employees might take a little more time with their work if they knew they were sure to get a job back if mistakes were found. In his analysis of the system Jim had found that many employees were aware of the *number* of documents they processed, yet they were not aware of their level of quality.

Jim also made some very specific changes in his own management style. His analysis showed that he paid much attention to errors, but gave little attention and few positive consequences for good performance. He now saw to it that over a 3-week period he spoke to each employee of each shift at least once about something good each one was doing: "Helen, Hal Prescott over in test engineering had some nice things to say about your drawings on the Alpha Project. I know they got the specifications to you late, but somehow you pulled it off. Things like that help the image of our whole department. Thanks." Or, "Bill, that layout looks fine. The templates are all labeled, and I see you've got the cross-codes all worked out. You know, we're putting together a manual on departmental procedures to use in training new employees and transfers. If you don't mind, I'd like to use this as a sample. I'll leave your name on it, if that's okay with you."

Simple words of recognition and encouragement were offered to provide feedback on good performance. Although Jim continued to call errors to the attention of certain individuals, now he also called attention to good things that were happening. After implementing these changes, Jim evaluated the results through continued tracking and comparison of these measures with the baseline data. The illustration on the opposite page shows the results of using recognition and encouragement to reinforce and strengthen good performance.

A definite improvement in productivity resulted in Jim's department from his intervention program. Although the amount of work completed dropped briefly at first, this eventually improved as well. However, knowledge of a successful project such as this does call several questions to mind.

How Long Can Such Results Last?

Results from using MBC techniques have been observed in many organizations for several years. In general, results will last as long as new procedures continue to be applied. When an engineer solves a problem in a manufacturing process or a service person fixes a machine, they are

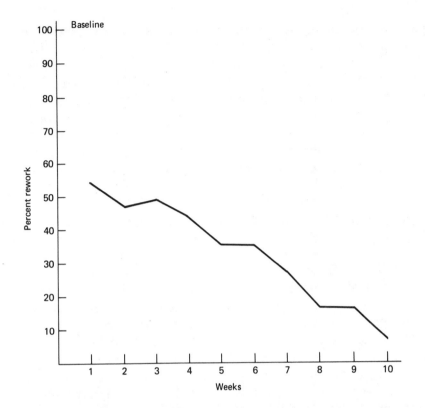

Percentage of Designs Requiring Rework

applying a technology to produce improvement. It isn't typical to ask, "How long can such improvement last?" As long as the technology is applied, the improvements will be maintained. Other problems may develop, but the technology isn't abandoned when this occurs. In fact, it is simply applied again to solve the new problem.

It is true that people are not machines, but people do behave lawful-ly. There is a "science" of human behavior, and when that science is applied systematically by a manager, that manager is using a technology. As long as you as a manager use the technology, other things remaining the same, you will continue to see improvement. And if other things do not remain the same, you can still continue to use the MBC technology; however, this time to deal with the changes.

Can MBC Be Misused?

If you fear that applying such a technology with people will lead to a harsh, mechanistic management style, consider what Jim did. His project is quite typical of how managers use MBC. He didn't tear people down; he built them up. When a service representative is called in to repair a malfunctioning computer, he cannot ignore the physical laws that have produced the machine failure. It would be inappropriate to blame the machine for not working (e.g., it has a bad attitude, is lazy, or unmotivated). You might be amused to think of the service representative bullying the machine or threatening it with dire consequences if it didn't improve. It's not so amusing to think of managers behaving that way with employees, but unfortunately many do.

Far from MBC possibly leading to the improper treatment of employees, the system is specifically designed to prevent such mistreatment. MBC provides managers with alternatives to blaming, threatening, and bullying.

Could a technology be misused? Yes, of course. The very same technology that helps doctors to save lives can help others to design terrifying weapons of bacteriological and germ warfare. Yet the very nature of MBC encourages managers first to consider their own practices and how these practices might be influencing employee performance. When used by an entire organization, MBC focuses the organization's attention on the work environment it is providing for its employees. Managers and organizations using MBC will look first to their own practices and procedures when analyzing poor performance, rather than automatically blaming employees. When intervening to produce change, MBC encourages reinforcement-oriented approaches that absolutely require managers to show respect for the individual and, in fact, to be sensitive to each individual's uniqueness.

Will MBC Work on All "People Problems"?

Despite its obvious advantages, MBC is not a panacea for solving all problems. It is a simple, down-to-earth, concrete approach that helps managers to be more effective in the all-important area of people-management. Although not necessarily the only approach, MBC certainly deserves to be part of the repertoire of skillful managers as they perform their job of solving problems and encouraging good performance—as they carry out their responsibility of getting work done through people on a daily basis.

Does MBC Simply Mean "Praise"?

Ah, but what about productivity? Will a manager who is using MBC be "giving the shop away"? Will she tell everyone they are great, regardless of performance? Is MBC just praising people, no matter what they do? No, this is not how it works. MBC illustrates the importance of specific, honest, sincere feedback on both good and poor performance. As you will see in Chapter 3 and from the many case histories in this book, the effectiveness of MBC projects is often measured by the impact they have on traditional measures of performance and productivity in an organization. Beginning with Chapter 3 you will begin to develop your own action plan for testing the efficacy of MBC in your own work setting.

SELF-TEACHING EXERCISE

Self-Quiz

1. List the five steps that comprise the MBC approach.

2. What words did Jim use at first to describe his particular problem?

3. When Jim became more specific in describing his problem, what words did he use?

4. From simply reading Jim's case history, what would you say the step of pinpointing is all about?

5. In general, how would you sum up the change procedure employed by Jim?

6. How long can results obtained by using MBC procedures last?

Answers

1. a. Pinpoint
   b. Track
   c. Analyze
   d. Change
   e. Evaluate
2. Jim used the words "lazy," "bad attitude," "unmotivated," and "didn't care."
3. Jim used the words "making mistakes."
4. Pinpointing has to do with being more specific (see Chapter 3).
5. Jim provided more feedback by having people correct their own errors. He provided encouragement and recognition for good performance.
6. As long as MBC procedures continue to be applied.

SELF-TEACHING EXERCISE

Try This:

Think about a current problem with a person or group of persons. It may be a concern you have with a subordinate, a fellow supervisor or manager, your boss, or some other significant person in your life. Perhaps you have a concern about a child or spouse. In the space provided, describe the problem in a few brief sentences. (You will be referring back to these descriptions later in the book.)

Individual #1 _____ (Name) _____
Problem Description

_____

Individual #2 _____ (Name) _____
Problem Description

_____

Individual #3 _____ (Name) _____
Problem Description

Individual #4 _____ (Name) _____
Problem Description

_____

CHAPTER THREE
PINPOINTING

What is your most serious concern regarding an individual with whom you must work in your organization? Think for a moment of someone with whom you find it unpleasant to work. What is it about that person that makes working with him or her so unpleasant? What words come to mind? Before going any further, take a sheet of paper and write down five words or phrases that best describe the person you have in mind.

Does your list contain any of the words shown in Table 1? If it does, then your concerns match those of thousands of other managers. But how do you begin to focus on these concerns?

What Is Pinpointing?

Pinpointing is a skill that helps managers translate their general concerns into specific, measurable behaviors. Once these behaviors have been specified objectively, you have taken the first step toward improving the situation. A common problem among managers and executives is that they tend to talk in generalities—they don't get down to specifics. On the other hand, MBC does not deal in generalities; it deals only with specifics.

Pinpointing is the skill of describing someone's performance (including your own) in specific, objective, measurable terms. If you think that sounds pretty simple, you're right. But you would be surprised how many supervisory personnel could benefit from some training and practice in this area. The following conversation is typical of many managers and executives:

"Duane, you say Steve is a problem employee. What exactly seems to be the problem?"
"Well, he's so negative all the time."
"What makes you say he has this negative attitude?"

TABLE 1 **Some Words Often Used by Managers to Describe Unsatisfactory Employees**

Unmotivated	Doesn't care
Lazy	Too aggressive
Negative	Perceptually impaired
Bad attitude	Unsophisticated
Immature	Childish
Lacks confidence	Not creative
Insecure	Rigid
Defensive	Bitter
Big ego	Stupid
Dumb	Short tempered
Naive	Shy
Insubordinate	Disagreeable
Disruptive	Lacks drive
Careless	

"Well, he's so lazy."

"Lazy?"

"Yes, he just doesn't seem to care about his work."

"What do you mean, 'he doesn't seem to care'?"

"Well, he's just a real problem employee."

If you get the feeling there isn't much progress being made, you're right. The reason is that Duane is using *labels* to describe Steve. Labels do not lead managers to take specific action to improve things, and moreover, they're often unkind. Pinpointing involves avoiding labels, and instead, talking about the actual behavior that led to the label in the first place. Listen now as Duane attempts to sum up his thoughts just prior to completing his annual appraisal of Steve's performance:

"Well, Steve is just plain disagreeable. He's unmotivated, stubborn, aggressive, and a generally disruptive influence. In fact, there are times when he's plain insubordinate. I think he has poor perceptual ability, and he certainly doesn't seem to think rationally half the time. He's immature and has poor reasoning power. I think he's intelligent enough, but he lacks motivation and drive."

Hopefully, no one on your team is as badly off as Steve; however, some managers speak up right after hearing a description like this to say they have a Steve working for them!

Frankly, I don't know of any psychiatrist, psychologist, physician, personnel specialist, or any other professional who would know where to begin with such a long, vague, discouraging list of problems. A major problem with most of the words used by Duane is that they do not suggest a line of action for improvement. His words are merely labels. They might communicate a general picture (at least you know not to let Steve transfer into your department), but we don't know from the labels what concrete steps to take that will help Steve improve. Labels do not lead to solutions.

Where Do Labels Come From?

Labels originate from three main sources:

- *Labels come from the "rumor mill" or from old appraisal forms:* Managers often get an informal verbal report from another manager about an employee transferring into their department: "I'd look out for Joe if I were you; he's got a real attitude problem." Occasionally, a poorly executed written appraisal will attempt to "net out" or summarize the strengths or weaknesses of an employee. Words such as "drive," "motivation," and "attitude" appear and are then repeated by successive managers.
- *Labels are used when a manager sees employees doing something they should not be doing:* A group of young employees hired by a company was assigned to a testing operation. Their performance was excellent. It was so good, in fact, that by 2:00 p.m. they had finished the work it had taken the previous team all day to finish. With nothing else to do, the young workers began to tell jokes to pass the time. They laughed loudly and the sound carried over a partition, disturbing another supervisor and her team. With time on their hands, this group of employees also wandered out into the warehouse and over to an administrative center, distracting some other employees in the process. Within only a few days these young men had acquired the labels of being immature and having a bad attitude.
- *Labels are used when a manager fails to see employees doing something they should be doing:* A programmer, new to a department, was observed staring out the window for long periods of time. His manager reported that she saw him daydreaming. The words "lazy" and "unmotivated" seemed appropriate. Imagine her surprise when his first three projects were all delivered under deadline, with far fewer lines of computer code than projected, fewer test shots needed for troubleshooting, and shorter run times than expected required. The programmer had been thinking about his work when he was observed by his manager. As thinking is one of the highest functions human beings can perform, the manager realized her error in using such labels as "unmoti-

vated," "daydreamer," and "lazy," especially after viewing the results of this employee's mental efforts.

Knowing the sources of labeling can help you to avoid labeling and start pinpointing instead.

How to Stop Labeling and Start Pinpointing

Two ways to accomplish this are:

- If the label comes from the rumor mill, toss it out. Confirm performance for yourself.
- If the label comes from seeing or failing to see an individual do something, back off from the label and be specific. Talk about the behavior that you saw or failed to see—the behavior that led you to use the label in the first place.

Listen again to Duane after he has had some training and practice in pinpointing. He is still talking about Steve, but the difference is that now he is being specific and objective:

"Well, almost every time I discuss a new project with Steve, he argues and complains about the workload. He tells me why the job can't be done or shouldn't be done.

He's been late about eight times in the last month, and he overextends his lunch hour and coffee breaks. I've spoken to him about it informally, but he refuses to even acknowledge that it's a problem and says he needs more time anyway.

At staff meetings he's often verbally abusive toward other team members, calling their proposals 'stupid' or 'dumb' and attacking them personally rather than focusing on the technical aspects under discussion. At other times he will come out with distracting one-liners, jokes, and sarcastic comments.

He broke company rules at least three times last month, things like smoking in a nonsmoking area, parking in a safety zone, and bringing food into a nonfood computer area.

When he makes group presentations using an overhead projector, he may have to switch each transparency around three or four times before it's in the proper orientation. In addition, his presentations are poorly organized. He dwells on detail, and no one seems to know where he's going. When someone asks him a question, instead of just answering, he'll usually come up with some cute phrase or joke.

And it's the same thing with his reports. On one standard report he keeps getting the sequence mixed up. He may start working on one report, then stop and pick up in the middle of another. Sometimes data even show up on the wrong reports. And, as if that wasn't enough, they're usually turned in 2 or 3 days late.

When he's involved in staff work, analyzing a problem for upper-level management, he often forgets to ask the crucial questions.

He refuses to take part in any of the training programs that would help him get promoted."

Steve is not necessarily any more desirable an employee now, simply because his manager is being specific, but at least Duane is no longer groping around with only vague generalities to work with in describing Steve's inadequacies.

The exercise that follows gives you an opportunity to match the specific, pinpointed behaviors with the labels Duane originally used. The eleven labels Duane used are shown on the left. Read over his statements about Steve to find the pinpointed behavior or behaviors that match each label. For example, Duane labeled Steve as "disagreeable." The matching pinpointed statement is that Steve "argues and complains." Compare your answers with Table 2, which contrasts the words Duane used before pinpointing with those he used after mastering the skill.

SELF-TEACHING EXERCISE

Match the Pinpointed Behavior to the Label

Before:	*After:*
"Steve . . . ."	"Steve . . . ."
1. Is disagreeable.	1. Argues and complains.
2. Is unmotivated.	2.
3. Is stubborn.	3.
4. Is aggressive.	4.
5. Is a disruptive influence.	5.
6. Is insubordinate.	6.
7. Has poor perceptual ability.	7.
8. Doesn't think rationally.	8.
9. Is immature.	9.
10. Has poor reasoning power.	10.
11. Lacks drive.	11.

Why Bother to Pinpoint?

Whereas few managers would know where to begin with the discouraging, vague, general words listed on the left in Table 2, for every

TABLE 2 **The Words Duane Used to Describe Steve Before and After Being Trained in Pinpointing**

Before:	*After:*
"Steve . . . ."	"Steve . . . ."
1. Is disagreeable.	1. Argues and complains.
2. Is unmotivated.	2. Is late and extends coffee breaks.
3. Is stubborn.	3. Refuses to acknowledge lateness and argues about it.
4. Is aggressive.	4. Calls proposals stupid or dumb.
5. Is a disruptive influence.	5. Makes jokes and is sarcastic.
6. Is insubordinate.	6. Breaks company rules, e.g., about smoking, parking, etc.
7. Has poor perceptual ability.	7. Switches overhead transparencies around.
8. Doesn't think rationally.	8. Does not organize presentations and reports.
9. Is immature.	9. Uses cute phrases and jokes.
10. Has poor reasoning power.	10. Mixes up the sequence on reports and forgets to ask crucial questions.
11. Lacks drive.	11. Refuses to participate in company training programs.

pinpointed behavior on the right there are documented case histories describing how managers have faced these problems and solved them using MBC procedures. You may not like or agree with a particular manager's approach, but at least you will understand the scientific principles of human behavior that led him or her to try the technique(s) selected. Many organizations are pulling together individual MBC projects and case histories into compendiums and resource guides to be used in training both new and experienced managers. Similar projects appear in Appendix 1.

This is not to imply, however, that MBC is a "cookbook" management approach, for instance, "Here's what Bill did to reduce a high scrap rate. Why don't you try the same thing?" Rather, MBC is a system and a set of principles to help you arrive at your own solutions to performance problems, solutions geared to the uniqueness of the individuals who report to you or with whom you are working. An old maxim is analogous to the way MBC can be used: "Give a man a fish and he will eat for a day, but teach a man to fish and he will eat for the rest of his life."

The case histories in this book are meant to illustrate, not to suggest a rigid, lockstep imitation of the specific procedures used by others. Skillful managers using this approach will most often be able to custom-design better procedures than others could suggest for them, because these managers alone are intimately familiar with their own situations and employees. But the common thread that ties together all MBC procedures is the five-step process and a science of human behavior.

However, the key to it all is pinpointing. The pinpointed behavior is the equivalent of the card catalog in the library or the key identifiers and descriptors in a computer search and information retrieval system. Pinpointing behavior is the entry-level skill required for the proper use of MBC. Only if you pinpoint can you be sure everyone is talking about the same problem. Managers and supervisors using MBC are often encouraged to find that performance problems for which they are being held accountable have been experienced by others, that it's not the first time employees have come in late, missed deadlines, used the company phone for personal business, had high rework or error rates, or the myriad of other problems that beset supervisory personnel.

SELF-TEACHING EXERCISE

An Exercise in Pinpointing

To acquire some experience in pinpointing, focus on some problems in your own work setting. Refer back to the description of current problems you wrote at the end of Chapter 2. For this exercise you may want to use one or more of those problems or concerns. The behavior or aspect of performance you select can be something inappropriate or undesirable. However, you might also think of some good thing that goes on at work, some people you like or admire.

What Behavior Can You Pinpoint?

Behavior is "anything of a physical or verbal nature that people do." Walking, talking, answering the phone, making a presentation at a meeting, driving a truck, assembling parts on an assembly line, and writing a computer program are all examples of behavior. Everything that occurs in an organization is the result of someone's behavior. However, two general classes of behavior are of concern to managers.

Work behavior is the behavior found in job descriptions, performance plans, and organization charts. Work behavior consists of the various tasks people carry out and is most often the performance organizations pay employees to accomplish.

Another category of behavior is also of concern to managers—*interpersonal behavior*. Interpersonal behavior consists of those behaviors or actions that appear in no job description, performance plan, or organizational chart. Interpersonal behavior includes slamming doors and phones, rude and crude remarks; personally abusive statements; critical, sarcastic remarks, grimaces and frowns; hurling papers across the room; refusals to work with other employees; and temper tantrums. On the other hand, interpersonal behavior also refers to behaviors you would like to see more of: smiles, cheerful greetings, words of appreciation, expressions of interest in someone's work, seeing another's point of view, and encouragement of others. When examining interpersonal behavior it is most important that this behavior be *performance related*. Business organizations have come a long way in the past 20 years in understanding that employees have a right to their own interpersonal styles, including manner of dress, personal habits and customs, and even the way a job is done, as long as quality and quantity of work do not suffer. Most sophisticated organizations stress employees' personal rights in their management training programs. The widespread use of performance planning and objective appraisal programs is consistent with a move toward fairness and objectivity in assessing performance. MBC, and particularly pinpointing, is consistent with this movement.

Interpersonal behavior that is performance related refers only to those behaviors that have a direct impact on some measurable product or outcome of the organization. For example, in an MBC workshop a production control manager was trying out the pinpointing skill. "Paul," he said, "how about this one? I've got a guy who works alone most of the day in a parts bin area filling orders that are then taken by employees to the manufacturing floor. Now, every time I go out to see him, he's humming and singing tunes from shows and operettas. Is that pinpointed?" Yes, it is. But the manager was quick to add that he had no desire to change the behavior; in fact, he realized the humming and singing might even be helping the employee. It was an interpersonal behavior, but in this instance it was *not* performance related.

To contrast, move that employee out of the parts area into the organization's corporate offices or to division headquarters. Give him a desk close to some other employees and a new title. If he continues humming and singing in this new environment, then his manager probably will be concerned about this behavior. It is this type of performance-related interpersonal behavior on which you should focus.

There is, of course, an area of overlap between work and interpersonal behavior, and some pinpointed behaviors of concern to you may fall into this category.

Whose Behavior Can We Pinpoint?

MBC is an influence model to guide your interactions with individuals at many levels in your organization. In the space below list several different people in your organization whose behavior affects you.

Include those people whom you wrote about at the end of Chapter 2. Next to each person's name indicate whether that person is:

A. An employee or subordinate reporting to you
B. A peer manager or supervisor at your level
C. Your manager or the person you report to
D. Some significant other person with whom you must interact to get the job done

Person	Role
1. *Bill Johnson*	*B*
2.	
3.	
4.	
5.	
6.	
7.	
8.	

These are people with whom you must interact in order to carry out your job successfully. They are the people you must often influence as part of accomplishing your work.

Your Employees or Subordinates

Managers report that they are concerned about a wide variety of pinpointed employee behaviors. Not all are negative. From a problem-solving point of view, however, some that concern them include coming to work late, making errors, frequently complaining about and criticizing other employees, missing deadlines, and not completing work. The pinpointed behavior of concern to you may be exhibited by one individual or several.

Your Peers

Some managers report that their employees are the least of their problems. Their concern is often with fellow first- or second-line managers, those at the same level as themselves in the organization. You can probably think of a peer-level manager or executive with whom it is a delight to work. You enjoyed the last project you worked on together and look forward to the next. What is it specifically about that person's behavior that gives you these feelings? On the other hand, managers sometimes report that they have peers who seem determined to destroy the work of another manager's team. These individuals pursue their own responsibilities with such rigidity that no one wants to work with them. You would probably avoid such peers and circumvent them whenever possible. Even when these fellow managers have legitimate goals and are trying to influence you, they do it in such a way that you end up feeling alienated and upset.

Your Manager

A person who is very important to you in the organization is your manager. Middle- or upper-level managers exhibit a wide variety of pinpointed behaviors in an organization. On the positive side, first-line managers report such desirable behaviors as providing clear-cut instructions or outlines of a task, obtaining the resources a first-line manager needs to get a job done, and returning phone calls promptly. Unfortunately, some behaviors of upper-level managers can also negatively affect the performance of others, including such behaviors as using threats and coercion; assigning the same task to two or three first-line managers, thereby creating confusion and "turf" problems; giving unclear instructions; and jumping over one or two lines of management and giving direction to employees without notifying the manager involved.

Significant Others

Finally, you may interact with a group of individuals who are not actually part of your department or organization, but who are important to it and to you—significant others. These are people in another part of the company who provide services to you or use your services. They may be outside vendors of services to your team or your company; contract service firms doing building cleaning and maintenance; or food service firms, suppliers, advertising agencies, and consultants. It may be part of your job to influence the performance and behavior of individuals in such firms.

A PINPOINTING EXERCISE

Having seen *what* behaviors you can pinpoint and *whose* behavior you can pinpoint, try out this new skill. Using Table 3, write down at least four specific pinpointed behaviors of concern to you. The phrase "of concern to you" is intentionally broad. Managers and supervisors are concerned about both good and poor performance. You may like to see some pinpointed behaviors maintained or increased. From your standpoint these are *desirable* behaviors. On the other hand, you may like to see other behaviors decrease in frequency or stop entirely. These are *undesirable* behaviors. Remember, MBC is not an approach to be used just in crises or with "problem employees." Many managers use the MBC system to ensure that hard-working employees do not become "turned off" to their jobs.

Space is provided for pinpointing both desirable and undesirable behavior. You need not fill in all of the boxes, but carrying out the exercise will help you to focus on *specific* behaviors of concern to you in your organization. Once you have pinpointed them, you will be able to see how MBC can help you.

Now Check Yourself

If you have completed this exercise successfully, the words you have written on the pinpointing form will satisfy the following criteria:

1. *A pinpointed behavior describes something someone is doing or saying.* It is *observable* behavior. If your written statement meets this criterion, good! However, if words like "drive," "attitude," "uncommunicative," and "unwilling" still appear, take a moment and try to revise the statement so that it describes *observable* behavior. For example, "drive" might be reworded to "He arrives early, produces twice as much as his peers, and he doesn't take breaks."
2. *A pinpointed behavior can be counted or measured in some way.* If the behavior described on the pinpointing form is in fact a pinpointed

TABLE 3 **Pinpointing Form**

DESIRABLE	UNDESIRABLE
Employee(s)	Employee(s)
Peer(s)	Peer(s)
Manager(s)	Manager(s)
Significant other(s)	Significant other(s)

behavior, it is directly observable—it can be counted. I am not suggesting you *would* measure it, but simply that you *could* if you so chose.

If you are still not sure whether you have properly pinpointed a behavior, you might ask a friend to check your statements against the criteria provided.

Something to Avoid

One thing to keep in mind when first pinpointing is: *Avoid interpretations and explanations of why the pinpointed behavior occurs.*

Interpretation and explanation are, of course, key factors to a manager's success. But a good diagnostician does not jump too quickly down one avenue of interpretation or explanation, but rather attempts to consider objectively all the evidence before reaching a decision.

The failure to maintain objectivity might cause you to ignore a crucial fact and thereby misdiagnose the problem. One manager pinpointed an employee's behavior by saying, "Stan checks in with me eight or nine times each day to show me how he's progressing and to ask if he's still on the right track. I think he checks with me so often because he's insecure and doesn't have confidence in his own judgment." The second statement is an interpretation—an attempt to explain why Stan checks in with his manager so frequently. The manager was assuming and inferring the cause of the pinpointed behavior.

It should not be assumed or inferred that an undesirable behavior is totally the fault of that person. For example, a manager might pinpoint the behavior of "missing deadlines on nine out of eleven reports over the last 3 months." Now that is a pinpointed behavior. But if the manager then goes on to state "and it's because he doesn't care," this assumes that the reports are late because of a lack of caring. That may be so, but there may also be several other causes of this behavior. When pinpointing, focus only on the behavior. Not until you get to the step of *analyzing* why people behave as they do should you consider the causes of pinpointed behavior. Once you have pinpointed a behavior of concern, you can use two specific analytical tools to determine why these behaviors are occurring and how you can intervene to decrease undesirable behaviors and increase desirable ones.

Now That You've Pinpointed

If your statements on the pinpointing form met the suggested criteria, you have successfully taken the first step in using the MBC approach. You are focusing on specific, concrete, observable behavior.

You have avoided making unwarranted—and often unjustified—assumptions as to why these behaviors are occurring. The question now remains, "Is the pinpointed behavior *truly* performance related?" This serves as a final check in determining whether an attempt to change behavior would be legitimate and ethical. Despite all the emphasis placed on the relationship of the pinpointed behavior to performance, managers sometimes realize after pinpointing that they are focusing on a nonperformance area. A job may be carried out in a particularly flamboyant way that the manager does not particularly like, but it is nevertheless carried out. A person may speak slowly and hesitantly, but this may not at all affect his performance. If it does not, then MBC recommends that you not pursue it further. Stop trying to change that particular behavior of that individual. It is his or her own business, and none of yours. And if you have not been appraising this individual at the level deserved or have been giving smaller salary increases simply because of this nonperformance-related behavior, you may have some thinking to do and changes to make regarding your management techniques.

One manager criticized an employee for "lacking a sense of urgency." When he finally pinpointed the behavior that was bothering him, it turned out that the employee always walked very slowly around the department and in the building. He never walked quickly or "hustled." Yet all his work was accurate and completed on time. In addition, his record of attendance and punctuality was excellent. The employee had no problem. The manager did. The manager decided to stop any attempts to "change" the employee.

If, however, a behavior directly affects an individual's responsibilities and the needs of the business, as well as his own credibility and career opportunities, then you are focusing on an area of legitimate concern and it would be appropriate to continue. The illustration on page 36 outlines the decision-making process involved in the pinpointing skill of MBC.

Pinpointing leads to this first-choice point in the MBC decision-making process. You will learn more about the decision-making process in Chapter 4, Tracking.

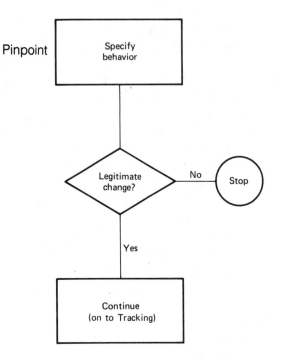

Pinpoint

Specify
behavior

Legitimate
change?

No

Stop

Yes

Continue
(on to Tracking)

The MBC Decision-Making Process:
Pinpointing

CHAPTER FOUR
TRACKING

The next step in using the MBC approach is tracking: tracking the frequency of the pinpointed behavior itself or tracking some product or output produced by the pinpointed behavior. Almost everything that is accomplished in an organization is accomplished through people. The total goods and services produced by a company are the result of individual behavior in that organization. Unloading a shipment of parts and raw materials, expediting the material to a manufacturing floor, pushing the buttons on computers and machines, packing the final product, preparing and sending invoices to customers, paying for raw materials, and negotiating the contracts needed to do business are just a few of the thousands of behaviors that make up the workday. It is this behavior for which managers are held responsible. Often, the outcome of these behaviors is used in measuring and evaluating a manager's skills. Most organizations may already be tracking much of this behavior, but may not be using the information properly. The axiom, "If you can't measure it, you can't manage it" has relevance. The ability to simply measure a resource does not guarantee that it will be well managed; however, measurement does increase the likelihood of good management.

Why Track?

The MBC system uses carefully, precisely measured behavior and outputs in organizations for three important reasons:

- Tracking allows you to ascertain the current level of performance to decide how serious a problem is or how well someone is performing.
- Tracking provides a baseline against which you can compare later results and thus assess the effectiveness of your intervention procedure.
- Tracking may become a key part of the "change" procedures you ultimately use to solve a problem.

How to Track

If a behavior is pinpointed correctly, you will have no problem tracking it. In fact, if it represents a concern about performance, you have been tracking it already, although probably in a haphazard manner. In most cases, when a manager is concerned about an individual's performance in a group that manager is reacting to the observed or perceived frequency with which certain pinpointed behaviors occur. Some behaviors occur too often while others do not occur often enough.

You know that occasionally employees will be away from their workplace; however, if you try to find an employee eight times in one day and six of those times you cannot, the frequency of absence is judged to be excessive. Some reports will always be late, but a certain frequency of late reports will cause a manager to react negatively. When you think about it, a manager can use only two things to appraise the performance of another individual accurately:

• The actual pinpointed behavior as it is occurring, or
• The product or output that is a direct result of the pinpointed behavior

In addition, a manager has a choice of type and frequency of measurement:

• A manager can track *continuously*, measuring all the behavior or product, or
• A manager can *sample* and measure only some of the behavior or product.

These tracking methods are illustrated below.

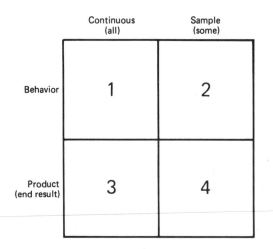

	Continuous (all)	Sample (some)
Behavior	1	2
Product (end result)	3	4

The Four Methods of Tracking Performance

Some Examples

A manager reported that a professional employee "lacked confidence" and was "insecure." When he pinpointed the behavior that had led him to attach these labels, it became apparent that the employee frequently came into the manager's office to ask questions. Because this behavior always occurred in the manager's presence, it was no problem to track all of it; therefore, tracking method 1 (behavior-continuous) was used to see just how often the question-asking behavior occurred. Was it really excessive? Was it out of line with the amount of time the manager spent with other individuals? What constituted "out of line"? Managers must ask these crucial questions. How are you judging others? Tracking often forces you to examine honestly the techniques you are currently using to assess the work performance of others.

A supervisor felt that one inspector working in a quality control department was "lazy" and "unmotivated." However, the pinpointed behavior was allowing substandard parts to slip through the inspection process. Because the supervisor saw the inspector only once or twice a day, she was not able to observe the actual behaviors involved. In fact, what she was reacting to was the *product* of the behaviors, that is, substandard parts that slipped through inspection. Realizing that a sample might not provide an adequate measure, the supervisor decided to document every substandard part for 1 week, wherever it showed up (usually in final test or at a customer location). Therefore, she used tracking method 3 (product-continuous) to determine the seriousness of the problem. She also decided to monitor simultaneously the substandard parts allowed to slip through by all other inspectors in the quality control department, so she could see whether the inspector in question really was performing less satisfactorily.

Practicality and ease should determine what particular tracking method is used. What will work? What would be easiest? What seems most practical? Sometimes it will be easier to track a product; at other times, a behavior. Remember, however, that a pinpointed behavior is the source of the problem, even when products or output are being tracked. If you ultimately seek to produce improvement, it will be through changing behavior.

Decisions Based on Tracking

In many cases tracking may demonstrate to a manager that the problem is not as serious as first anticipated or that an employee is not doing any less than others with similar job assignments. It may also alert the manager to the fact that no standards exist or that standards have not been communicated clearly to the employee. If so, a manager should remedy these situations first before assuming that the problem rests with the employee and is caused by lack of motivation or "laziness."

The drawing below illustrates the next decision to be made after tracking has been carried out properly. A manager should now decide whether the frequency of the problem justifies further effort. Sometimes it is simply not worth the effort to try to change a behavior because

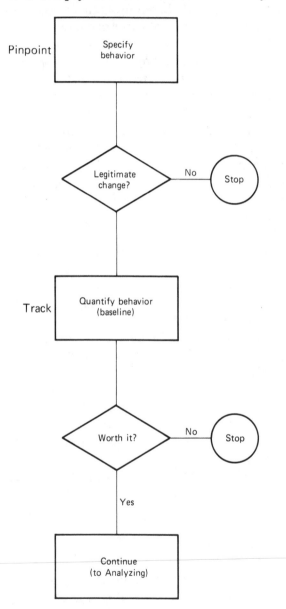

The MBC Decision-Making Process Through Tracking

the cost far outweighs the benefits. However, if you decide that the problem is serious enough to warrant improvement, you should move to the next step in MBC—analyzing.

Complete the following exercise using the pinpointed behaviors of concern to you that were entered on page 21.

1. Take each behavior you pinpointed and transfer it to the first column of the tracking form shown below.
2. Specify the tracking method in the second column.
3. Specify *what* will be tracked, along with *where* and *when* the tracking will take place, in the last column.

Tracking Form

1. Write the pinpointed behavior of concern in Column 1.
2. Specify the tracking method in Column 2.
3. Specify *what* will be tracked, along with *where* and *when* the tracking will take place, in Column 3.

    1. Behavior—continuous tracking (all)
    2. Behavior sampling (some)
    3. Product—continuous tracking (all)
    4. Product sampling (some)

1. Pinpointed behavior	2. Tracking method	3. (a) What, (b) Where, (c) When
Making specific recommendations for expenditure ceiling as part of monthly financial report.	3	*(a) Number of specific recommendations for each division or site location* *(b) On monthly financial report* *(c) Each monthly deadline date*

Once you have completed the tracking form, you should actually do some tracking over a period of 1 to 2 weeks. Try it. You can use this information later to develop an action plan.

Possible Problems with Tracking

The moment the issue of tracking or measuring human behavior comes up, we are immediately on guard as to possible pitfalls and dangers. This is appropriate. We would not want to ruin relationships it has taken years to develop by instituting a new measurement system that creates more problems than it solves. It must be emphasized that the proper use of MBC does not involve keeping surreptitious records on people's behavior and then suddenly jumping on them with "Ah-hah! Gotcha!"

Although measurement is fundamental to MBC, it does not have to be measurement conducted without an employee's knowledge—nor will it be in most cases. From a scientific standpoint, it might be nice to establish before and after measures. However, the average manager is concerned about working with people effectively, not conducting scientific experiments. The only reason a working manager might measure a behavior without an individual's knowledge would be to see if the problem was really as serious as he or she anticipated. Most supervisors and managers who have used MBC techniques have demonstrated good judgment and practiced the simple rule "When in doubt, leave it out" in deciding whether it was appropriate to track some behavior without the knowledge of the employee involved.

You have probably seen measurement misused in organizations. The pejorative term *bean counters* is ample testimony to the resentment and fear expressed by many about some tracking procedures. Is it the tracking itself or the way the numbers are often used that produces resentment? If the only use a manager or organization makes of tracking is to find deviations and then threaten or punish those who deviate, then tracking will be resented. Many employees welcome measurement as a tool when it is used properly to evaluate, provide feedback, and reward performance.

CHAPTER FIVE
ANALYZING WHY PEOPLE BEHAVE THE WAY THEY DO

Why people behave as they do is a crucial question for managers. Your hypotheses about why people do what they do often determine the actions you will take as you attempt to influence them. Knowing *why* things happen is important in many areas. For example, when a service representative is called in to solve a problem with a piece of office equipment, think of the sequence of actions taken in this process. First, the representative asks questions to ascertain the specific problem (pinpointing). Then he tries to determine the frequency of failures or the magnitude of the problem (tracking). But how would you react if the next thing he did was dive into the back of the machine, make a few haphazard adjustments, yank out a few modules, bang the machine a few times, and say, "Well, that might help! Why don't you try it for a few days and see if anything I did solved the problem?"

You would most likely be quite disturbed at the service representative's random approach. You know that some systematic cause is producing the machine failure and you have a perfect right to expect the service representative to take the necessary time to conduct diagnostic tests to locate the cause of the problem. You would further expect that once the cause is determined, action will be taken that is consistent with what has been learned about the problem; and that the service representative will make systematic changes to improve the equipment's performance.

But what happens when people do not perform as expected in organizations? Frequently a manager will jump in and haphazardly begin to make changes, hoping something will work. The manager may try to convince, cajole, counsel, coach, embarrass, threaten, or frighten employees into changing their behavior. But there is a better way. By using MBC you can objectively analyze and audit human performance systems. The results of these analyses and audits can often lead you directly to systematic changes in the environment (not in people's hearts, souls, or minds) that may produce improved work performance.

Some Managerial Hypotheses

To understand why people behave as they do, consider the behavior of a traffic control officer in downtown Pittsburgh (captured on film by Allen Funt for one "Candid Camera" program). The traffic officer is not merely standing quietly giving the standard hand signals, the behavior we are accustomed to seeing at intersections. Instead, when a motorist begins to inch forward in spite of a red signal, the officer adopts the stern expression of a parent disciplining a child, and with one hand on his hip he uses the other to shake a scolding finger at the motorist. The policeman gets his message across. When another car moves too slowly, the officer places his hands against his nodding head and pretends that he is falling asleep from boredom. Should a motorist appear upset at the heavy traffic, the officer takes up an imaginary violin and imitates a musician playing a soothing melody. And when motorists move swiftly across the intersection, they do so to wild applause from the officer. However, if a pedestrian moves too slowly, the officer clasps his hands together as if in prayer and beseeches them to cross the street more quickly. Occasionally he takes a pedestrian's arm and has a brief conversation with that person as he escorts him or her to the other side of the intersection. Throughout all of this activity the officer punctuates his antics with hops, skips, jumps, and exaggerated facial expressions.

Before continuing to read, use the space provided to complete the following statement: In my opinion the police officer behaved the way he did because

Compare your answer to those given by other managers and supervisors: he enjoys his work; he's happy; he's creative; he's bored; he's getting attention; he's an extrovert; he's highly motivated; he's unhappy; it's effective; he's self-actualized; it's his personality; he likes people; he's insecure about people and this is a defense mechanism; he was trained to do it that way; he has a good attitude; he has a bad attitude; he has strong ego needs; he has drive; he's paid to do it that way.

Well, that's certainly a healthy number of suggestions! Table 4 illustrates how these ideas can be logically organized.

Table 4 **Some Reasons Given to Explain Why the Police Officer Behaves as He Does**

The officer:

Enjoys his work.	Gets attention.
Is happy.	Is effective.
Is creative.	Is trained.
Is bored.	Gets paid.
Is an extrovert.	
Is unhappy.	
Is self-actualized.	
Has personality.	
Likes people.	
Is insecure about people.	
Is motivated.	
Has a good attitude.	
Has a bad attitude.	
Has ego needs.	
Has drive.	

What differentiates the list on the left from that on the right? The list on the left contains suggestions for causes of human behavior that tend to be from *inner* or *internal* forces. These forces are subjective to the extent that you cannot observe them directly. You can only infer or assume that these causes exist; you have no means of verifying that the statements on the left truly represent the *causes* of human behavior. You could, of course, ask the police officer whether he was bored, happy, motivated, and so on, but his verbal report might or might not be reliable. Sometimes people don't even fully understand their own internal feelings.

On the other hand, the list on the right contains statements related to causes of human behavior that are *outer* or *external*. These causes reside in the external environment. Most managers understand that the environment can have a powerful influence on behavior. The causes on the right are objective in that you can actually observe, test, and conduct experiments to ascertain the extent to which they are influencing behavior. Because these causes are concerned with real events, no inferences or assumptions need be made. You can simply observe and conduct experiments to determine whether they are, in fact, affecting behavior.

For example, what about attention? Are people giving the police officer attention for his behavior? You can answer this question by monitoring the number of people who look or smile at him. (You know a "Candid Camera" crew took the trouble to film him!) How many people talk to him about his "performance"? Are articles written about him in the local newspaper? What if you placed him at an intersection with fewer people to look at him, or if you asked people not to smile? You would quickly find out whether or not attention was a factor in his behavior.

Is the officer effective at his job? Certainly you could compare the traffic flow at his intersection with traffic movement at equally busy intersections. How does traffic flow on his day off or when he has a replacement? How much time elapses between his giving a hand signal and someone responding to his instruction? Is this response faster or slower than that achieved by more traditional instructions? How many accidents occur at his intersection? How many pedestrians are knocked down? What if you staged a few fender-benders? Would the officer suddenly change his style of directing traffic?

Perhaps he *was* trained to conduct himself this way. You could check his personnel file or interview his superior officer. Some causes of behavior can be verified; others cannot. There may, of course, be some interaction between forces in each list; however, you can only verify or test those statements contained in the list on the right in Table 4.

How Do You Know What Causes Behavior?

An interesting observation can be made about the list on the left in Table 4. Some of the hypotheses are obviously mutually exclusive. The officer is either happy or unhappy; he can't be both. Yet each one seems to be a reasonable assumption. He is either enjoying his work or he is bored. His attitude is either good or bad. Because you have no means of observing these forces directly, you cannot ascertain which one(s) are having an effect. Yet experienced managers have observed the same behavior and performance and developed widely divergent views such as these concerning the cause of that behavior. It is little wonder then that the actions managers take to change and improve behavior are equally divergent. If everything managers did to effect behavior change worked equally well, there would be no problem. However, all procedures do not work equally well; in fact, some procedures can harm employees. Because you may never know which or how many of the proposed internal causes are truly operative, the list on the left does not appear to have a great deal of potential for suggesting systematic ways of changing behavior.

On the other hand, the list on the right is quite specific. If you wanted to change the police officer's behavior or help other officers to behave like him, knowing the cause of his behavior becomes important. Even though you might initially propose a number of potential causes, because all refer to *external* events you would be able to determine quickly which one(s) were operative. You could then change that particular aspect of the environment and watch to see if the officer's behavior changed. Or you could provide that critical aspect of the environment for other traffic officers and watch to see if they then behaved in a similar way.

Managers can attempt to find out why people behave as they do by observing, interviewing, and experimenting in order to relate outer environmental factors to work performance. This is the purpose of the *A-B-C Analysis*, the first of two MBC tools for analyzing why people behave as they do.

Some Things to Think About

Before you learn how to use the A-B-C Analysis, keep in mind several questions that are concerned with the two main areas managers point to when considering why people behave as they do—inner and outer forces.

1. In which area do you think employees (and managers are employees too) would be comfortable having a manager exert influence? Internal? External? Or a combination of both?
2. As a manager, where do you feel most confident, competent, and comfortable working? On internal forces? External ones? Or what proportion of time in each?
3. When you consider the tools your organization has given you to assist in managing human behavior, where are those tools designed to work? On internal causes? External ones? Or to what extent in each area?

These questions will become increasingly relevant as you continue to learn about the techniques of MBC.

SELF-TEACHING EXERCISE

For each of the following statements indicate whether someone's behavior is being attributed to an inner, unobservable cause or an outer, observable cause.

	Inner, unobservable cause	Outer, observable cause
1. Bill is often late because he's unmotivated.	_____	_____
2. Ann's success is due to her drive.	_____	_____
3. Charlie stayed home because an auditor came from headquarters.	_____	_____

	Inner, unobservable cause	Outer, observable cause
4. The programmers didn't make flowcharts because they're hostile.	_____	_____
5. The warehouse workers made fewer errors because their individual results were posted daily.	_____	_____
6. The mechanics worked slowly because they didn't care.	_____	_____
7. Robin showed up at the meetings because her boss was there.	_____	_____
8. The sales representatives made their quotas because they were self-starters.	_____	_____
9. The sales representatives made their quotas because of the 10 percent bonus they received.	_____	_____
10. Gene greeted everyone who came in because of his positive personality.	_____	_____
11. The assembly-line workers made suggestions about quality because they had good attitudes about their work.	_____	_____
12. The assembly-line workers made suggestions about quality because their supervisors implemented many of their suggestions.	_____	_____
13. The airline pilot spoke to passengers in a slow, deep voice because he had confidence.	_____	_____
14. The airline pilot spoke to passengers in a slow, deep voice because he had heard other pilots speaking that way.	_____	_____
15. The store clerk suggested additional items to the customer because she was trained to sell that way.	_____	_____

Answers

1. Inner 2. Inner 3. Outer 4. Inner 5. Outer 6. Inner 7. Outer 8. Inner 9. Outer 10. Inner 11. Inner 12. Outer 13. Inner 14. Outer 15. Outer

CHAPTER SIX
CONDUCTING AN A-B-C ANALYSIS

Remember the computer programmer who complained so often to his manager? Consider that case history for a moment to see how the use of MBC, and specifically, the A-B-C Analysis helped that manager.

At first the manager described the programmer as "highly negative" and having a "bad attitude." After learning how to pinpoint he became more specific and began to focus instead on the behavior of complaining. You may recall that the programmer complained about working conditions, other employees, other managers, the pension plan, the weather, and so on.

The manager decided that this behavior was performance related because it was hampering the programmer's relationships with other people as well as with the manager himself. The manager felt that he could not assign the employee to train others or lead a project because all he would do is complain about these people. The individual's behavior was affecting his "promotability" and career opportunities in the company adversely, and yet he had expressed a desire on more than one occasion to become a manager.

An informal tracking phase helped the manager determine whether the behavior was occurring as frequently as he thought, and whether the programmer was actually complaining more than other department members. After tracking the behavior he found that on some days the programmer "collared" him as many as eight or nine times just to pass on some bad news. Based on this quantified information, the manager decided the problem was worth examining further, and that it would be worth the effort if the employee decreased his complaining behavior. It should be emphasized that the manager in no way wanted simply to suppress the complaining. He was fully aware that he could do that just by telling the employee to mind his own business, but occasionally the employee did identify a work-related problem that helped the manager to improve departmental operations. Knowing it was crucial to continue receiving the information he needed, the manager was not about to cut himself off from an important source. However, he did want the employee to discriminate between work-related criticisms and general "backbiting, moaning, and griping." To this end he used the A-B-C Analysis.

The A-B-C Analysis helps managers to concentrate on a very important principle of human behavior. This principle states simply that *behavior is influenced by the environment.*

The A-B-C Analysis Shows Why People Behave the Way They Do

The fact that behavior is influenced by the environment is a key concept and basic principle of the MBC system. An A-B-C Analysis helps managers realize to what extent behavior is actually influenced by environmental factors.

Another reason for using the A-B-C Analysis is that a strange thing sometimes happens to the labels that managers tried to do away with when they learned the skill of pinpointing. This strange thing is that the labels often pop up again as the manager struggles to understand why a pinpointed behavior is occurring. A typical exchange might go something like this:

Manager: "Ned is just a problem employee."

Me: "What do you mean?"

Manager: "Well, he's got a real attitude problem."

Me: "Do you think you could try to pinpoint the actual behavior that leads you to say that Ned has an 'attitude problem'?"

Manager: "Oh, yeah—pinpointing. Okay. What I mean is that more often than not he's late to department meetings, and he misses some of them altogether."

Me: "Good, that's a pinpointed behavior. Now, do you have any idea how often this happens?" (Focus on tracking.)

Manager: "Well, not exactly, but there's no question he misses at least one meeting a week, and I'd say he's late for about 80 percent of the others."

Me: "Fine, that does seem like a problem it would be worth examining. Do you have any idea why he's coming late and missing some of the meetings?"

Manager: "Sure!"

Me: "Why?" (I eagerly anticipate a precise answer based on the behavioral approach I've been discussing with the manager.)

Manager: "He does it because he has an attitude problem."
  I sigh, smile weakly, and suggest we take a break for coffee, realizing I may be reinforcing the manager for an undesired response.

Imprecise terms, such as "attitude," "motive," and "drive" sometimes jump from being labels that are stuck on employees as descriptive terms to being explanatory labels for forces *inside* employees. Managers are paid to describe what their employees do and also to explain and understand why they are doing what they are doing. Unfortunately, managers often use labels both to describe and to explain employee behavior. Pinpointing eliminates vague descriptive labels and an A-B-C Analysis omits explanatory ones.

Antecedents and Consequences

Two critical features of the environment are the antecedents and consequences of any behavior. Antecedents are events that occur *before* the pinpointed behavior that is being analyzed. Consequences are events that occur *after* the pinpointed behavior.

The programming manager began completing an A-B-C Analysis form, as shown below.

A	B	C	Probable or known effect
Antecedent	Behavior	Consequence	of consequence
	Complaining		

He then considered what events immediately *preceded* the complaining behavior. He concluded, "As far as I can recall, if you walk up to him, he starts complaining." He then added that information to the analysis form.

A	B	C	Probable or known effect
Antecedent	Behavior	Consequence	of consequence
Walk up to him	Complaining		

The form immediately suggests an environmental change the manager could make that would probably lead to a decrease in complaining: don't walk up to him and he won't complain. But obviously this is not a realistic solution to the problem. It is the company's policy that managers be available to employees, and besides, as the manager pointed out, "After a while he'd probably learn to track me down or just complain to my boss." Although avoiding employees who complain frequently is not a practical solution, some managers or supervisors do "solve" the problem this way.

Realizing that an antecedent change was not reasonable, the manager instead turned his attention to the consequence column of the analysis. As he gave some thought to the first thing that occurred immediately *after* the behavior he realized, "I listen to him," and entered this on the form.

A Antecedent	B Behavior	C Consequence	Probable or known effect of consequence
Walk up to him	Complaining	I listen	

"But I'm not going to stop listening!" he exclaimed. "That's part of being available to our employees, and besides, once in a while I hear something I need to know!" Because he didn't want to stop listening after the employee complained, the manager considered what else happened soon after the behavior occurred: "Well, I think he complains so much because he's insecure and lacks confidence, so I try to reassure him that he's doing a good job."

The manager inferred that such factors as "insecurity" and "lack of confidence" were causing the complaining, so what did he do? He attempted to reassure the programmer by praising his efforts. When the programmer complained about the performance of another department that interfaced with his own, the manager's response was: "Well, I know they often don't get the precoding done on time and there are errors. But that's a different group under another division. I'm working on it. Don't worry, I know you're doing a good job; I know when they slow you down. Just keep up your end." Following complaints about fellow employees, the manager might say something like, "Look, that's my problem. You try not to worry about their performance. You're doing fine, just keep up the good work."

The manager began to realize that each time the programmer complained, the complaint was followed by a reassuring statement. He thought, "Maybe, just maybe, my reassurances are making the problem worse." For the first time the manager was examining a new hypothesis, the possibility that his attempt to solve the problem (reassuring the programmer) was actually serving to encourage the complaining. The manager's A-B-C Analysis form now looked like this:

A Antecedent	B Behavior	C Consequence	Probable or known effect of consequence
Walk up to him	Complaining	I listen	Reinforces behavior
		I reassure him	Reinforces behavior

How could the manager test this new hypothesis? Simply by changing the consequence of reassuring the employee and watching to see the effect of this change on his complaining behavior. The manager decided he would listen quietly when the employee complained, but he would not reassure him. Instead, he might request specific documentation, suggestions for solutions, or ask what steps the programmer might take to solve the problem himself. In response to nonwork-related complaints, he would simply shrug his shoulders. At the same time the manager recognized the importance of not cutting the employee off from all positive feedback. If the reassurances were in fact encouraging the complaining behavior, then why not use the reassurances to encourage desirable behavior?

In the following weeks the manager made a point of stopping to talk with the programmer whenever he saw him busy at work or helping others. He gave credit and reassured him, but only as a consequence of appropriate behavior. Within about a month he was able to report a significant decrease in frequency of complaints and a marked improvement in his relationship with the employee. The number of complaints did not drop to zero, but those he made were relevant, the kind of problems the manager needed to know about.

What an A-B-C Analysis Demonstrates

A properly conducted A-B-C Analysis illustrates several key facts:

• *The A-B-C Analysis shows how managers' actions are affected by their hypotheses about why people behave as they do:* As long as the manager "thought" (hypothesized/inferred/assumed) that the programmer complained because of "insecurity" and "lack of confidence," he would take action consistent with that hypothesis. In this case the action taken was to reassure the employee.

- *The A-B-C Analysis helps managers identify new hypotheses to explain why people behave as they do:* Because hypotheses as to why people behave as they do often lead to action, if you lengthen the list of hypotheses, you will probably lengthen the list of possible actions you can take to improve the situation.

- *The A-B-C Analysis forces managers to consider how the environment may be affecting the individual concerned:* Instead of automatically assuming that a problem in performance lies *within* an employee, managers can now consider how the environment may be impeding good performance. The A-B-C Analysis may show that the environment is actually encouraging poor performance.

This simple analysis demonstrates the power that consequences have in affecting behavior. The two key processes through which consequences exert this power are called *reinforcement* and *punishment*.

Reinforcement

Reinforcement is the process through which certain consequences strengthen the behavior they follow. Consequences that encourage the behavior they follow are called *reinforcers*.

Punishment

Punishment is the process through which certain consequences weaken the behavior they follow. Consequences that discourage the behavior they follow are called *punishers*. You can tell if a certain event or action is a reinforcer or punisher by the effect it has on the behavior it follows. A manager who uses these consequences effectively to change a behavior is either *reinforcing* or *punishing* that behavior.

To gain practice in discriminating between reinforcement and punishment in the MBC sense, consider how these words are defined operationally by the effect they have on behavior. First, look at the effect reinforcement and punishment have on the behavior of a manager, as shown on page 55.

A Antecedent	B Behavior	C Consequence	Probable Effect (Reinforcement or Punishment)
Empty boxes, old printouts and litter in the work area	The manager requests that employees clean up the work area.	The employees comply and the work area is cleaned.	?

What effect do you think the consequence of a clean work area had on the manager's behavior? Do you think the manager would be likely to request that the employees clean up again if empty boxes, old printouts, and litter were to accumulate in the future? If your answer is yes, then you are saying that the consequence of a clean work area would maintain or increase the likelihood that the manager would request the employees to clean up, that is, it is a reinforcer.

At this point you are only guessing. The true test would be to see what the manager did the next time the same antecedent condition presented itself. To determine whether a particular consequence is a reinforcer or punisher for you, ask yourself, "In a similar situation (antecedent condition), would I act the same way again?" If the answer is yes, then the consequence was a reinforcer. On the other hand, the answer might be, "No, having experienced that consequence, I would not behave the same way again. I would try to deal with the situation differently." In this case the consequence would be considered a punisher.

Table 5 illustrates nine other A-B-C sequences that often affect managers and executives. Read through each and write the word "reinforcement" or "punishment" in the probable effect column. As you work through the exercise, put yourself in the place of the manager engaging in the behavior. The first sequence in Table 5 has been completed for you.

Compare Your Answers

Compare your answers with those of other managers who have analyzed these particular sequences.

Incident 2. The most prevalent response here is "punishment." In their honesty and candor managers admit that, although they're not happy about it, this kind of consequence occurs all too often: "It's such a

TABLE 5   **A Self-Teaching A-B-C Analysis Exercise (Understanding Managers' Behavior)**

Antecedent	Behavior	Consequence	Probable Effect (Reinforcement-Punishment)
1. Empty boxes, old printouts, and other papers litter the work area.	The manager requests that employees clean up the work area.	Employees comply and the work area is cleaned.	Reinforcement
2. Empty boxes, old printouts, and other papers litter the work area.	The manager requests that employees clean up the work area.	Employees argue and complain and gripe about working conditions in general.	
3. You're floating a new idea you believe will improve business.	You bounce the idea off your counterpart in another plant.	Your colleague is enthusiastic, offers to help, and says that he can provide you with supportive data.	
4. You're floating a new idea you believe will improve business.	You bounce the idea off your counterpart in another plant.	Your colleague says he has some problems with it, and besides that he thinks they tried it once and it didn't work.	
5. The second-level manager requests a monthly status report.	The first-level manager complains about a lot of pressure and misses the deadline.	The second-level manager is sympathetic and backs down from the deadline (for the third time).	
6. A stack of papers on your desk requires dictation.	You dictate replies to your secretary.	You have a clear desk.	
7. 10:15 a.m.	The manager walks into Department A.	The employees greet the manager cheerfully and report that work is progressing well.	
8. 10:30 a.m.	The manager walks into Department B.	The manager is told the workload is too heavy, and listens to several complaints and gripes.	

TABLE 5 (cont.)

			Probable Effect *(Reinforcement-* *Punishment)*
Antecedent	*Behavior*	*Consequence*	
9. The first-level manager has an idea.	She goes into the third-level manager's office to discuss her proposed idea.	Before she can begin, the third-level manager starts discussing "pressing problems," "concerns," and "troubles." The third-level manager then assigns additional work to the first-level manager.	

hassle, it's easier to get someone else." "I leave it for the second shift." "I do it myself." Employees teach managers how to behave all the time. Proper understanding of MBC principles can help managers, if only out of self-defense, to obtain a better understanding of the influence employees have on their behavior. Far more managerial behavior is "controlled" or influenced by employees than most people would be comfortable admitting. MBC can help clarify the mutual influence managers have on employees and employees have on managers.

Incident 3. Most managers write the word "reinforcement." They say they would be back, that the consequence would encourage their behavior.

Incident 4. Many managers write "punishment" here, meaning that they know from experience that after a while, in similar situations, they have stopped talking to certain individuals. However, some managers write "reinforcement." They say, "I may not like it, but I do keep going back. It is in such discussions that I hear the negatives. I need to know the negatives so I don't get 'blown out of the water' by upper management." This response indicates that these managers are applying the definition of reinforcement accurately. They are not responding on a "like/dislike" or "pleasant/unpleasant" basis; they are correctly using the criterion of "Will I do the same thing again, in a similar situation?"

Incident 5. The majority of managers write "reinforcement" as their answer here, acknowledging that middle management is responsible for the behavior and performance of first-line management and supervisory personnel. Too often a second-line manager may "teach" a first-line manager an undesirable behavior.

Incident 6. Most managers write "reinforcement" for this example, indicating that for them completion of work is a reinforcer. They also acknowledge, however, that this is an area where what is reinforcing to managers might not be reinforcing to employees. When workers learn that the consequence for finishing a job is to be assigned a less preferred, lower-level task, they often learn to drag out the job until quitting time. Consider the following:

Manager: "By the way, when you finish those reports, I'd like you to clean out the stockroom."

Employee: "Sure." (thinking "Sure, but who says I'll finish the reports?")

On the other hand, skillful managers, those who understand the power of consequences, use them wisely to encourage desirable performance:

Manager: "Bill, these reports look fine. When you're finished typing them, I wonder if you'd like to take a crack at the new word processing equipment. You could try it out on that special project we've been working on; then you'll be able to help the rest of the department when they finally get a chance to use it."

Incidents 7 and 8. If you wrote "reinforcement" for example 7 and "punishment" for example 8, as most managers do, then you can see why some managers spend most of their time with their "good" employees and avoid the "bad" ones. You like to be around people who give you feedback on what a good manager you are. It is funny, though, how the hard-working, "good" employees become like that because of excellent managerial skills, and the less effective, troublesome employees get that way because of their "bad attitudes" and "lack of drive."

Incident 9. Many managers write "punishment" here, stating that in similar circumstances their upper-level manager has "turned them off," so they no longer initiate discussions. However, some write "reinforcement" because even though they don't get to express their own ideas they do learn about higher-level business issues. Again, the only way to be sure would be to track how many individuals continued to seek out their upper-level managers and how often.

You may disagree with how someone else completes the preceding exercise. When managers do not agree on whether a consequence is a reinforcer or a punisher, it is usually because of one of two simple facts:

• *Fact 1:* What is reinforcing to one person may not be reinforcing to another.

• *Fact 2*: What is reinforcing to one person may be punishing to another.

It serves no useful purpose to spend time arguing or philosophizing over what is or is not reinforcing. All you need to do is simply observe your own behavior and that of others to see how consequences are influencing the behavior they follow. Now you are ready to try an A-B-C Analysis on some typical employee behaviors.

Table 6 contains six A-B-C sequences that often affect employees. As with the previous exercise, read through each example and write the word "reinforcement" or "punishment" in the probable effect column. This time, however, put yourself in the place of the employee engaging in the behavior, and ask yourself how you think each consequence would affect you as the employee.

Compare Your Answers

Incident 1. Most managers write "reinforcement" here. They agree that although it is not a particularly satisfactory situation, it occurs all too frequently. Managers sometimes inadvertently teach employees to behave inappropriately.

Incident 2. "Punishment" is most often selected for this example. In this instance, punishment may decrease the behavior of walking over to the vending machine and buying a cup of coffee at other than assigned break times. However, the problem in this particular case is that the antecedent condition was also employee behavior. You might hope that the punishment would not affect the desirable behavior of exceeding production goals, but it probably would. This is just one of many problems created by the use of punishment as a technique for changing behavior.

Incident 3. If you wrote "punishment," then you understand why many employees do not adhere to certain safety routines. Their unsatisfactory performance in this area is not necessarily caused by a "poor attitude," but to the fact that environmental influences are either discouraging or failing to support the desirable behavior.

Incident 4. The sarcastic remark of the supervisor may indeed punish the employee for honestly noting that a count was missed. The next time the employee may be less likely to report events honestly and may instead enter false information on the record sheet.

TABLE 6   **A Self-Teaching A-B-C Analysis Exercise (Understanding Employees' Behavior)**

Antecedent	Behavior	Consequence	Probable Effect (Reinforcement-Punishment)
1. The manager requests that employees clean up their work area.	Employees argue and complain about working conditions in general.	The manager walks away, looking for someone else to clean up the area.	
2. Approximately 10 minutes prior to break time, an employee exceeds a production goal by 20 percent.	He walks over to a vending machine and buys a cup of coffee.	His supervisor reprimands the employee sharply for taking an early break.	
3. Fumes generated by a packaging operation require that goggles be worn.	The employee puts on her goggles.	The goggles fog up and obstruct vision, and other employees ridicule her.	
4. An employee forgets to note the total number of cigarette cartons packed in a 3-minute period, as required.	She notes on the record sheet that the count was missed.	The supervisor makes a sarcastic remark about the employee sleeping on the job.	
5. A blinking red light indicates excessive foreign material in computer chips on a manufacturing line.	A filter is changed in a mechanical feed line.	The blinking red light goes off.	
6. A bank branch office manager approaches a group of tellers.	The tellers report that everything is going well.	The manager says, "That's good to hear. Keep up the good work."	

Incident 5. Did you write "reinforcement"? Good! *Finally,* the environment is supporting appropriate, desirable behavior.

Incident 6. "Reinforcement?" Probably yes. But for what behavior? For the behavior of "reporting that everything is going well." Are things really going well? Who knows? They may or may not be. This example indicates the need for independent tracking systems so managers can be sure they are not simply reinforcing verbal reports of good work. Although it is important to reinforce timely verbal and written reports, you should also seek to reinforce accurate reporting.

This particular incident also brings to mind a complaint some managers make about their employees who "lack integrity" and are "dishonest." After pinpointing they say that these employees do not report problems as soon as they come across them. Instead they wait or say nothing at all until the small problem develops into a full-blown crisis. A simple explanation for why employees sometimes do not report problems to a manager is evident in the A-B-C sequence below.

Antecedent	Behavior	Consequence
An employee discovers a problem.	The employee reports the problem to the manager.	The manager frowns, raises his voice, looks exasperated, stomps around the office, says he has to do everything himself, that he can't trust anyone, etc.

It doesn't take much imagination to predict what the employee will do the next time he comes across a problem. Skillful managers who have learned to "manage by consequences" will reinforce honest, timely reporting, and then engage in joint, nonthreatening, problem-solving behaviors with the employee.

You can use the blank A-B-C Analysis form on page 62 to analyze pinpointed behaviors of concern to you. Transfer the behaviors from the Pinpointing form (Table 3, Chapter 3) to the Behavior Analysis form. Some suggestions for using the form follow:

1. When listing antecedents, focus on immediately preceding events. Look back at the examples in Tables 5 and 6. We are not looking for such things as "Passed over for promotion four years ago." You can't change that anyway. You are looking for initiating events or "triggers" for the pinpointed behavior.

2. Don't be concerned if you can't identify a reliable antecedent. Simply leave the column blank. This may indicate that some event is needed to serve as an antecedent to the behavior.

3. Feel free to list several antecedents and/or consequences for each behavior. Just be sure to indicate the probable effect of each consequence.

An A-B-C Analysis Form

Instructions: 1. Transfer the pinpointed behaviors of concern from the Pinpointing form to the Behavior column (column 2).
2. In column 1, list as many antecedents as you can think of for each behavior.
3. In column 3, list as many consequences as you can think of for each behavior.
4. In column 4, indicate the "probable effect" of each consequence.

Antecedent(s)	*Behavior*
The deadline for reports, including recommendations for action, arrives.	The employee turns in well-documented report, but does not include recommendations for action.
1.	
2.	
3.	
4.	

4. If you feel, after listing it, that a consequence is not a reinforcer
    or punisher, write "none" in the Probable Effect column.

Your completed A-B-C Analysis should illustrate how antecedents
and consequences are affecting the pinpointed behaviors of concern to
you. The A-B-C Analysis is an analytical tool for understanding why
people behave the way they do. Another analytical tool is called the
Balance of Consequences Audit. You will learn to conduct such an audit
in Chapter 7.

Consequence(s)	Probable Effect (Reinforcement-Punishment-None)
The manager makes recommendations.	Reinforcement

CHAPTER SEVEN
CONDUCTING A BALANCE OF CONSEQUENCES AUDIT

If you have been doing the suggested exercises you should have already discovered that MBC is not an approach to be used only for problem solving and troubleshooting. It can also help a manager to understand why an individual is performing satisfactorily.

In the previous chapter, we saw that an A-B-C Analysis can be used to relate desirable behavior to its antecedents and consequences, thus avoiding changes that may result in the suppression of good performance. We also saw how the A-B-C Analysis can be used to analyze undesirable behavior. In this case, conducting the analysis can help managers make changes to improve performance.

A true understanding of complex organizations and people, however, often requires the use of another analytical tool that delves deeper into the complexities of why people behave as they do. This MBC tool is called the Balance of Consequences (B-O-C) Audit.*

When to Use a B-O-C Audit

1. *Use the B-O-C Audit when you are analyzing the behavior of groups of people:* The A-B-C Analysis taught you that what is reinforcing to one person is not necessarily reinforcing to another. When all employees behave alike, a simple A-B-C Analysis may suffice. However, when some employees behave in one way and others differently the B-O-C Audit is needed.

*The term *Balance of Consequences* was first introduced by Karen Searles Brethower at the University of Michigan. Tom Connellan's *How to Improve Human Performance* (Harper & Row, New York, 1978), provides useful examples of how the Balance of Consequences affects work performance (pp. 101–105).

2. *Use the B-O-C Audit when individuals appear to be making a choice between desirable and undesirable behavior:* The MBC system teaches that people are rational. They do not behave randomly; rather, their behavior is prompted by certain antecedents and followed by certain consequences. If the antecedents are adequate and the consequences reinforcing, people will continue to behave that way. When a behavior changes, it is either because the current set of antecedents and consequences have changed or because people choose to exhibit another behavior that is being influenced by an even stronger set of antecedents and/or consequences. To understand why individuals are not doing what you want them to, it often becomes necessary as well to analyze why they *are* doing what they *want* to do. The B-O-C Audit is ideally suited for this purpose.

3. *Use the B-O-C Audit when both reinforcing and punishing consequences follow the same behavior:* In conducting the A-B-C Analysis earlier on the pinpointed behaviors of concern to you, you may have listed several consequences for one behavior. Some of those consequences may have been identified as reinforcers, others as punishers. But which seemed to be winning out and why? The B-O-C Audit will help you see why some consequences are stronger than others.

How to Conduct a B-O-C Audit

The following case history describes an organization that was experiencing a major behavioral problem with a group of employees.

The Case of the Programming Report Forms: A Performance Deficit Problem

A large corporation employs thousands of programmers and analysts to develop programs for internal use and also to develop software to sell to other companies. Government regulations, as well as business needs, require that employees in this area fill out and turn in programming report forms (PRFs) daily. These reports are logs of the type of work the employees are doing; they are used to determine how much of the employees' time is spent on "nonexempt," low-level programming activities and how much time is spent on higher-level, more professionally oriented "exempt" activities. One purpose of this report is to ensure that these professional salaried employees are paid for any nonexempt overtime. The company also needs the reports to estimate the cost of future development projects and to determine the mix of skills needed in present and future programming applications. If, for example, a team of three programmers spends 60 person-hours interacting with a user group, 200 hours actually writing lines of code (both exempt professional activities), and 90 hours in input/output activities (a nonexempt activity), the PRFs should reflect this.

Unfortunately, the PRFs are not being filled out properly or regularly. Many programmers report that it is an unnecessary nuisance. Some fill them out only when they receive a direct request from their managers. The managers report that they spend a number of hours each day trying to get the programmers to fill out the PRFs from the day before. Some programmers do turn the reports in regularly and on time, and the managers indicate that, if they have a chance, they try to express their appreciation to these employees. However, their busy routine does not allow much time for this activity.

One attempt to remedy the situation that is currently being applied is to have a second-level manager prepare a weekly list of the "worst" offenders for distribution to the various departments. These individuals may be scheduled for a meeting with the second-level manager. On a recent visit to one location, a management consultant heard cheering and clapping from the programmers when the list arrived and the names were read off.

Upon interviewing several of the employees, the management consultant heard some employees complain that they are not allowed enough time for filling out the PRFs and therefore must work late to total up the columns. Others complained that filling out the forms causes them to be caught in a traffic jam when they leave the office.

Programmers say that no one ever actually uses the reports to decide how to improve work groups. They state that the only response they get from upper management when they do fill them out is criticism for spending too much time on one type of activity or another. Some say they heard that an employee who filled out the PRFs honestly got a smaller salary increment than others who did not fill them out at all.

Management points to the fact that PRFs are necessary to comply with government regulations and to improve the scheduling of work, which in the long run will allow management to improve the programmers' wages and even give bonuses. The managers report that they hold stern counseling sessions with the worst offenders. They also report that on particularly hectic days they occasionally estimate what the programmers did and fill out the forms for them.

Now that you have read the case history, the five steps involved in conducting a B-O-C Audit are outlined in the sections that follow.

Step 1: Pinpoint the Desired Behavior

Focus here on the pinpointed behavior in which management would like the employees to engage. In this instance the behavior would be identified as "properly filling out the programming report forms daily." This pinpointed behavior is entered on the Desired Behavior line on the B-O-C Audit form, as shown below. (The behavior is desirable, at least from the standpoint of management.)

Step 2: Pinpoint the Undesired Behavior

On the line labeled Undesired Behavior, write the pinpointed behavior that is competing with the desired behavior, as the illustration on page 69 shows. This example focuses on the behavior that is the opposite of the desired behavior. However, a number of undesired behaviors could be competing for the employees' time. In addition, a sophisticated B-O-C Audit might also take into account other *desirable* behaviors that are competing for the programmers' time.

DESIRED BEHAVIOR: *Properly filling out PRFs daily*
_____

1.	2.
Reinforcing consequences	Punishing consequences

UNDESIRED BEHAVIOR: _____

3.	4.
Reinforcing consequences	Punishing consequences

IMPACT	TIMELINESS	PROBABILITY
Personal or Other	Immediate or Delayed	Certain or Uncertain

A Balance of Consequences Audit Form for the Programming Report Problem Showing Desired Pinpointed Behavior

DESIRED BEHAVIOR: *Properly filling out PRFs daily*

1.	2.
Reinforcing consequences	Punishing consequences

UNDESIRED BEHAVIOR: *Not filling out PRFs*

3.	4.
Reinforcing consequences	Punishing consequences

IMPACT	TIMELINESS	PROBABILITY
Personal or Other	Immediate or Delayed	Certain or Uncertain

The B-O-C Audit Form Showing Desired and Undesired Pinpointed Behaviors

Step 3: Track

At this point you can begin to measure the frequency of each pin-pointed behavior. Having done so, look at the ratio of desired to undesired behavior. Then, before going any further, decide whether it would be worth trying to change the behavior. If the decision is that it would be worth the effort, then move on to the next step.

Step 4: Identify and Categorize All Consequences that Are Influencing the Desired and Undesired Behaviors

You can see how the many complex consequences occurring in this case history were identified and categorized by managers involved with the PRFs case history in the illustration on page 70. This was accomplished by following these rules:

1. Those consequences that followed the desired behavior and appeared to reinforce it are written in column 1.

DESIRED BEHAVIOR: *Properly filling out PRFs daily*

1. Reinforcing consequences	2. Punishing consequences
Managers express appreciation *Comply with government regulations* *Improve scheduling* *Improve wages and bonuses*	*Stay late* *Caught in traffic* *Reports not used* *Criticism* *Smaller salary increment*

UNDESIRED BEHAVIOR: *Not filling out PRFs*

3. Reinforcing consequences	4. Punishing consequences
Managers fill out forms **Name on list/cheering and clapping* *Leave on time* *Larger salary increment* **Managers come around and request forms*	*Stern counseling sessions* **Name on list/cheering and clapping* *Poorer scheduling* **Managers come around and request forms*

*Indicates mixed-effects consequence (see text)

IMPACT	TIMELINESS	PROBABILITY
Personal or Other	Immediate or Delayed	Certain or Uncertain

The B-O-C Audit Form Showing Consequences as Categorized by Managers

2. Those consequences that followed the desired behavior and appeared to punish it are written in column 2.
3. Those consequences that followed the undesired behavior and appeared to reinforce it are written in column 3.
4. Those consequences that followed the undesired behavior and appeared to punish it are written in column 4.

Keep in mind that as you identify and categorize behaviors you are only guessing as to the probable effect of the consequences. You know when the consequences are occurring (either after the desired behavior or the undesired behavior), but you can only hypothesize as to whether a particular consequence is reinforcing or punishing. You will be able to confirm or reject your hypotheses only after you have carried out steps 4 and 5 in the MBC system and evaluated the results.

Note also that at least one consequence, "name on list/cheering and clapping," might legitimately be placed in two columns, indicating that what is reinforcing for some employees may be punishing for others. In the MBC system these are called mixed-effects consequences. For some employees these consequences work as planned, but for others they backfire. Mixed-effects consequences can create a new problem for each problem they solve. They are inefficient and the net effect on an organization is at best zero. They absorb a manager's time, yet they represent no additional value.

Step 5: Weight Each Consequence

Weighting each consequence involves determining the power a particular consequence has over a behavior. To better understand this step, briefly consider the variables that affect the power of consequences.

What Makes Consequences Powerful?

Four distinct variables affect the power that reinforcers and punishers have to influence behavior.

1. Magnitude (large or small)
2. Impact (personal or other)
3. Timeliness (immediate or delayed)
4. Probability (certain or uncertain)

The larger, more personal, more immediate, and more certain a consequence is, the greater will be its power over behavior. This is true for reinforcers as well as punishers. In contrast, consequences (both reinforcers and punishers) that are small, that affect others but not us, and that are delayed and uncertain to occur are weak and ineffective in influencing behavior.

Magnitude

Although the statement that magnitude affects the power of consequences makes intuitive sense, it is often difficult to quantify when comparing different reinforcing or punishing consequences. Unquestionably, a $500 suggestion award is greater in magnitude than a $10 one, but how do you compare the magnitude of a consequence like a manager's "expression of appreciation" with the magnitude of the consequence of "complying with government regulations"? It is true that you might conceive of a carefully controlled laboratory experiment that would enable you to make these comparisons; however, such techniques are not available or practical for working managers and executives. For this reason, the Balance of Consequences Audit does not attempt to measure magnitude directly. However, by dealing with the remaining variables of impact, timeliness, and probability, you will develop the skills needed to understand and become more aware of the magnitude of reinforcers and punishers in your own work environment.

Impact—Personal or Other

You can focus on the issue of impact by asking yourself, "Who is most directly affected by this consequence?" Consequences that directly affect the employees exhibiting the pinpointed behavior are classified as *personal*. Such consequences as a salary increase or bonus, a direct, verbal expression of appreciation, staying late, and being criticized would all be classified as personal.

Complying with government regulations or providing management with the information it needs for scheduling purposes are consequences that would be classified as *other*. It is not that other-type consequences are unimportant; they simply are not as important or powerful as personal ones.

Note that both reinforcing and punishing consequences can be classified according to impact. Although it may often be sufficient for managers to guess at the impact of consequences as they use the B-O-C Audit to troubleshoot a problem, it may also be possible to interview or survey the employees involved and have them rank or rate the consequences in terms of impact. In one organization, managers asked their employees to rate both the magnitude and impact of certain consequences on a seven-point rating scale.

The B-O-C Audit Form on page 73 shows how the managers involved with the programming report forms case history categorized the consequences they had identified in terms of impact: "P" representing personal, "O" representing other. If a consequence could in any way be conceived of as having a direct personal effect, it was categorized as "P." (In some situations, a midway "P/O" category helps resolve differences of opinion among managers.)

Timeliness—Immediate or Delayed

In real-life situations it is quite easy to measure the timeliness of a consequence. Simply ask yourself, "How long after the pinpointed behavior is exhibited does the consequence take place?" This time period of "latency" could be of any duration—from a few seconds to several years. In some organizations where the B-O-C Audit is used, managers are able to enter actual times.

Other things being equal, the longer the consequence is delayed, the less powerful its effect on a behavior. For most purposes, the following guidelines for determining timeliness apply:

1. *Immediate* consequences are those that occur within 1 week after the pinpointed behavior.
2. *Delayed* consequences are those that occur more than 1 week after the pinpointed behavior.

These criteria are flexible and can be changed to suit the circumstances. In some situations, immediate (I) is used for consequences occurring within 24 hours, immediate/delayed (I/D) for consequences beyond 24 hours up to 15 working days, and delayed (D) for those occurring past 15 working days. Precision is not always as important as the "feel" managers get for consequences by going through the audit. The form on page 74 shows how the managers weighted the timeliness of the consequences they had identified.

DESIRED BEHAVIOR: *Properly filling out PRFs daily*

	1.	2.
	Reinforcing consequences	Punishing consequences

Reinforcing consequences	Punishing consequences
Managers express appreciation P	*Stay late P*
Comply with government regulations O	*Caught in traffic P*
Improve scheduling O	*Reports not used P*
Improve wages and bonuses P	*Criticism P*
	Smaller salary increment P

UNDESIRED BEHAVIOR: *Not filling out PRFs*

	3.	4.
	Reinforcing consequences	Punishing consequences

Reinforcing consequences	Punishing consequences
Managers fill out forms P	*Stern counseling sessions P*
*Name on list/cheering and clapping P	**Name on list/cheering and clapping P*
Leave on time P	*Poorer scheduling O*
Larger salary increment P	**Managers come around and request forms P*
*Managers come around and request forms P	

*Indicates mixed-effects consequence (see text)

IMPACT	TIMELINESS	PROBABILITY
Personal or Other	Immediate or Delayed	Certain or Uncertain

The B-O-C Audit Form Showing Weightings of Impact

DESIRED BEHAVIOR: *Properly filling out PRFs daily*

1. Reinforcing consequences	2. Punishing consequences
Managers express appreciation P, D	Stay late P, I
Comply with government regulations O, I	Caught in traffic P, I
Improve scheduling O, D	Reports not used P, D
Improve wages and bonuses P, D	Criticism P, I
	Smaller salary increment P, D

UNDESIRED BEHAVIOR: *Not filling out PRFs*

3. Reinforcing consequences	4. Punishing consequences
Managers fill out forms P, I	Stern counseling sessions P, D
*Name on list/cheering and clapping P, I	*Name on list/cheering and clapping P, I
Leave on time P, I	Poorer scheduling O, D
Larger salary increment P, D	*Managers come around and request forms P, I
*Managers come around and request forms P, I	

*Indicates mixed-effects consequence (see text)

IMPACT	TIMELINESS	PROBABILITY
Personal or Other	Immediate or Delayed	Certain or Uncertain

The B-O-C Audit Form Showing Weightings of Impact and Timeliness

Probability—Certain or Uncertain

Probability is a measure of how likely it is that a consequence will follow a behavior. Again, this variable can either be estimated or actually measured. How often did the managers actually express appreciation? Are the programmers always caught in a traffic jam if they stay to fill out the PRFs? For most purposes, the following criteria for probability suffice:

1. Consequences that are *certain* are those that are likely to occur 80 percent or more of the time following a pinpointed behavior.
2. Uncertain consequences are those that occur less than 50 percent of the time following a pinpointed behavior.
3. A *certain/uncertain* category (C/U) is useful for those consequences that occur between 50 and 80 percent of the time.

DESIRED BEHAVIOR: *Properly filling out PRFs daily*

1.	2.
Reinforcing consequences	Punishing consequences
Managers express appreciation P, D, U	*Stay late P, I, C*
Comply with government regulations O,	*Caught in traffic P, I, C*
I, C	*Reports not used P; D, C/U*
Improve scheduling O, D, U	*Criticism P, I, C/U*
Improve wages and bonuses P, D, U	*Smaller salary increment P, D, U*

UNDESIRED BEHAVIOR: *Not filling out PRFs*

3.	4.
Reinforcing consequences	Punishing consequences
Managers fill out forms P, I, C	*Stern counseling sessions P, D, U*
*Name on list/cheering and clapping P,	**Name on list/cheering and clapping P,*
I, C/U	*I, C/U*
Leave on time P, I, C	*Poorer scheduling O, D, U*
Larger salary increment P, D, U	**Managers come around and request*
*Managers come around and request	*forms P, I, C*
forms P, I, C	

*Indicates mixed-effects consequence (see text)

IMPACT	TIMELINESS	PROBABILITY
Personal or Other	Immediate or Delayed	Certain or Uncertain

The Completed B-O-C Audit Form for the Programming Report Case

Check the illustration above to see how the managers weighted the consequences of completing and not completing the PRFs in terms of probability.

What the B-O-C Audit Shows

The precise weighting of all of the consequences in the B-O-C Audit is not as important as the sensitivity and awareness you develop as you carry out your own audit.

A properly conducted B-O-C Audit often reveals several patterns of a team that is not performing well or an organization that is experiencing problems. Some patterns that relate to the case history you have been working with follow:

• The reinforcing consequences for the desired behavior tended to be weak: many O's, D's, and U's were found.

• The punishing consequences for the desired behavior tended to be strong: note the number of P's, I's, and C's. Ideally there would be few punishing consequences for desired performance in organizations, but here they are many and strong.

On balance then, the weight of the consequences leaned in the direction of discouraging the very behavior the organization wanted to see—but that's not all:

• The reinforcing consequences for the undesired behavior tended to be strong: there were many P's, I's, and C's. Note how many of these consequences were actually created by management practices and procedures or by tradition.
• The punishing consequences for the undesired behavior tended to be weak. Although many were personal, notice how many were delayed and uncertain to occur. MBC does not advocate the use of punishment; however, the only thing worse than punishment that works is punishment that doesn't work, and that is precisely the result in this case history.

As you examine the audit it becomes clear that the reinforcers for the undesired behavior tend to outweigh the punishers for that behavior. Things are balanced—only in the wrong direction. At least four types of teams or organizations are depicted by a B-O-C Audit that is conducted properly. The figure on page 77 shows what two of these organizations look like in terms of how desirable and undesirable behaviors are reinforced and punished. These are "healthy" and "unhealthy" organizations, two of the four types of organizations that are discussed in the next section.

Types of Organizations Depicted by a B-O-C Audit

The Healthy Organization

In this type of organization the reinforcers for the desired behavior far outweigh any punishers that might discourage employees from engaging in desirable activities. Powerful punishers exist to discourage undesired behavior; however, it is unlikely that they will have to be used because the reinforcers for undesired behavior have been reduced to a minimum. In addition, the strong reinforcers for desirable behavior increase the probability that most of the day will be spent in useful, productive work. This desirable behavior therefore literally crowds out the time that might otherwise be spent in less desirable activities. There are only so many hours in a working day, and if an organization or individual manager creates an environment that supports productive

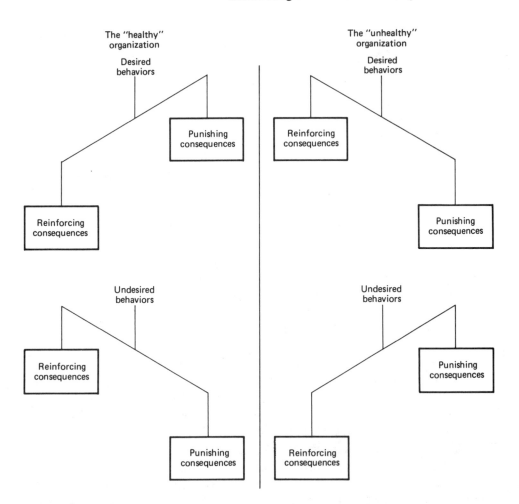

Types of Organizations Depicted by a B-O-C Audit—
Healthy and Unhealthy

behavior, most employees will prefer to engage in that behavior most of
the time.

The existence of strong punishers for undesired behavior means that
the good performers in a healthy organization will not become discouraged by seeing poor performers reap the same rewards. Strong punishers
in the MBC system, however, do not amount to cruel and unusual
punishment. In Chapter 8 we see just what these punishers are and how
they are used.

You might be thinking that "healthy" and "unhealthy" are labels,
and yet the MBC approach discourages the use of labels. However, some
labels can be operationally defined and only serve as shorthand for the
longer definition. The words "measles" or "mumps" are general labels for
some very specific physical symptoms. Similarly, the "healthy" orga-

nization is one in which reinforcing consequences outweigh punishing consequences for desired behavior and punishing consequences outweigh reinforcing consequences for undesired behavior.

The Unhealthy Organization

In the unhealthy organization the management team has mixed everything up, or at least has allowed everything to get mixed up. Managers may have forgotten that the most valuable resource in an organization is the human resource. Management may be focusing its attention on profits, shipping dates, the economy, and capital investment, but it most certainly is not directed at employees.

What actually happens in the unhealthy organization is that over a period of time good performers experience an increasing number of punishing consequences for their good work. This punishment of good performers may be in the form of having more work dumped on them because they are "the only ones who can be trusted," or it may be less direct, for example, budget cuts for a department that managed to cut corners and save money during the fourth quarter last year when corporate headquarters asked for voluntary belt-tightening. In the case of one department, the money saved was allocated to another manager who "accidentally" overspent his budget. And when the division vice-president saw that this department could "get along with less," he decided to make the cut permanent!

You probably have your own "horror story" that matches these. However, the problem with the unhealthy organization is not only that it is inefficient, but that it also destroys people. Bright, energetic, creative people come to work for this type of organization. They do not mind the lack of reinforcers provided by the organization because their reinforcement comes from a job well done. They take satisfaction in the quality of their contribution. Their first-line managers know these individuals do a good job, so do their fellow employees, and that's enough reward—for a while. Then, as they become more familiar with the organization, some of these hard-working employees begin to learn of another group of employees. These other individuals do the bare minimum to get by, feel bitter toward the company, have no use for management, and their work is poor in quality and quantity. But do you know what happens? These employees get some very "cushy" jobs. No one seems to bother them when they come in late, or not at all. The boss actually seems happier when they are not at work! And some of them are also getting above-average appraisals.

What the hard-working employees have begun to perceive is the mixed-up balance of consequences in this company. Not only is there little or no punishment for undesired behavior, but the employees who engage in such behavior are actually being reinforced for their poor performance. The good, energetic employees, however, are still undaunted. They are made of sterner stuff: "So what! If that's the way some people want to live their lives, let them! I wouldn't be able to face myself in the mirror every morning if I ripped off the company the way they do."

On the other hand, some of the good performers now decide not to agree to every single request: "I have a lot of things to do, and I'm not going to waste my time and hurt my own productivity by making up for someone else's mistakes." Also, for the first time, these individuals now allow something to go wrong without fighting to correct it: "Maybe that will teach the company to straighten out those turkeys in the Business Office!"

Despite this, the good performers still do an honest day's work for an honest day's pay. Until one morning they come in to find that their office has been moved without their being consulted, or that a new, boring, time-wasting administrative task has been assigned to them because the "other" department couldn't keep up with the workload, or any one of a dozen other ill-thought-out, poorly implemented management decisions. The practice turns out to be "the straw that broke the camel's back." In addition to everything else, the organization is now instituting procedures that inadvertently punish desired behavior. Management may say, "We didn't intend to punish anyone; it was just an administrative change." But MBC shows that it is not "intentions" that affect behavior; it is the consequences management provides that affect behavior. As a manager you cannot always predict whether a consequence will work as a reinforcer or a punisher, but the behavior of employees will show you immediately.

So the good, energetic employees are no longer so good and energetic. In fact, they are starting to look a lot like those bitter employees they began to be aware of several years ago. If their organization doesn't change, there will soon be no difference at all between the older and the newer employees. "Well," some may say, "that's because they're getting older. We all know that the longer you're with an organization, the less satisfied you become." We do? Is that always the case? Of course not. Why should age and length of service work that way? The answer is that they don't always. It is simply that in unhealthy organizations age and length of service are correlated with mixed-up consequences. Managers who are unaware of the tremendous impact that the environment has on behavior assume that such changes are due to age, length of service, a bad attitude, lack of motivation, and so on.

Two other types of organizations whose balance of consequences is less than perfect are shown in the next illustration.

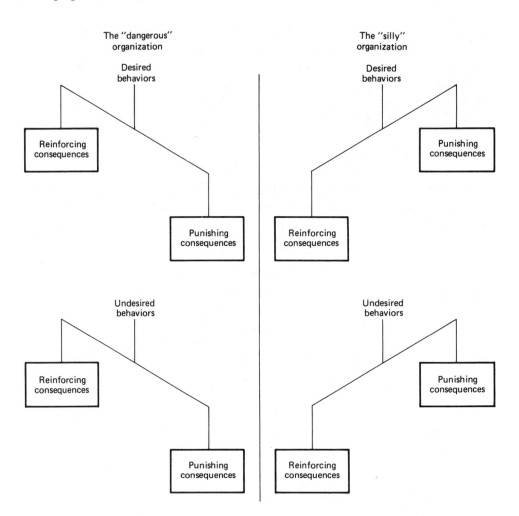

The "dangerous"
organization

The "silly"
organization

Types of Organizations Depicted by a B-O-C Audit—Dangerous and Silly

The Dangerous Organization

The "dangerous" organization is one in which the punishing consequences outweigh the reinforcing consequences for both desirable and
undesirable behavior. This organization can be harmful to your health—
both mental and physical. It is coercive, repressive, and out to get you. It
is most likely a company that can draw on a large labor pool where
employees must work to eat, to support themselves and their families,
and therefore have no choice but to stay. The variable that exercises the
most control over employees' behavior is fear of losing their paychecks.

Managers in such organizations exhibit high rates of verbal criticism, sarcasm, and ridicule. They are expert at using such procedures as ostracism, assigning undesirable tasks, and threatening termination. The organization's book of rules and regulations, which lists punitive measures for violations, rivals the *Encyclopaedia Britannica* in size and specificity of detail. Management has thought of literally everything an employee could possibly do wrong (some pretty good ideas for embittered employees here!) and has concocted a suitable punishment for each infraction.

What about the good performers in this type of organization? "That's what they're paid for." "They're supposed to do that—it's their job." "Why should I tell them they're doing good work when it's what I expect from them anyway?" Good performers get the same harsh treatment as poor performers—no favoritism here. Thankfully, however, fewer and fewer such organizations and managers survive.

The Silly Organization

The "silly" organization is a fun place to work. You get reinforcers for both good work and poor work—it really doesn't matter. No one bothers you except to smile and tell you that you're doing great, even if you're not. Nonprofit government agencies and institutions are often found in this category. The only one who suffers, of course, is the taxpayer, patient, student, automobile licensee, or other user of the services provided by the organization. If you just happen to come across one of the good performers who is currently being reinforced for good performance (you have a random chance!), this is all well and good. However, it may be just your luck to run into one of those individuals who is being reinforced for poor performance. He is smiling and happy, but your tax bill makes no sense and he doesn't know how to help you—and he doesn't care!

Or how about the hospital? "You didn't get your painkiller at 2:00 a.m.?" Too bad! "You were up all night? You rang for the nurse and she said she'd be right back, and she never came? Well, don't worry, we'll get it right tonight."

Or college? "You say the transcript you requested us to send in support of your scholarship application never arrived? Well, we have no record of your request. Oh, you have your cancelled check showing we received it? I see. Well, fill out this form and we'll try again. Oh, it's too late? You missed the deadline?" Too bad!

A silly organization can also be found among profit-making businesses where one or two products or product lines are so lucrative that they carry or support an entire group of unprofitable products and endeavors. Such businesses can afford silliness—at least for a while.

What Now?

Is the B-O-C Audit (and the A-B-C Analysis, for that matter) just a fancy way of saying "I have a problem"? No, it is more than that—much more!

Keep in mind that no statement in the B-O-C Audit should be a vague generalization, such as "communications problem." No statement in the audit alludes to some ephemeral theory: "If they only self-actualized more!" Each statement or consequence listed in the B-O-C Audit is a specific event, an event created by or under the control of management. Most of the consequences entered on the audit are a result of current management practices, procedures, or traditions. For this reason, the action needed to improve things becomes quite obvious. You don't need to change the hearts, souls, and minds of the employees, but you do need to change consequences. Changing consequences means changing management practices, procedures, and traditions. You know how to do that; you've probably been doing it for years, albeit somewhat haphazardly.

MBC helps you to see what changes might be necessary by focusing on the actual causes of both good and poor performance. Changes can thus be logically based on a system of problem solving. Because you are dealing with measurable, pinpointed behaviors and you know how to track them, you will know if the changes are working. The proper use of MBC helps to prevent problems and avoid going off randomly in a dozen wrong directions.

If you are attempting to solve problems, an understanding of MBC, and particularly, the use of such tools as the A-B-C Analysis and the B-O-C Audit, can help you in troubleshooting by getting you to focus on the specific areas and procedures that need attention.

In the next chapter you will learn what techniques are available to help you make desired changes.

CHAPTER EIGHT
CHANGING THE
ENVIRONMENT TO
CHANGE BEHAVIOR

March 5, 198_

Gentlemen:

We are exploring ideas for pamphlets, posters, bulletins, buttons, slogans, and so on that will contribute to increased morale, team spirit, job satisfaction, and productivity.

Your company may have a product, service, or even a promotional concept that could be useful in improving morale and fostering team spirit.

If so, please send us a catalog or a brief description of your products. Thank you.

Sincerely,

Signed by the Training Director

This letter is typical of the many frequently received in my office. Here we are, coming to the end of the twentieth century, and organizations continue to seek "pamphlets, posters, bulletins, buttons, slogans, and so on" to change employee behavior! Well, at least they are not looking for better coercive methods to improve productivity.

In one company the chairman of the board decided to eat with workers in the company's main cafeteria. He received quite a "welcome" from the cafeteria workers, also company employees. A few ice cubes quickly brought down the temperature of the chairman's soup to where the workers thought it deserved to be. The salt in his sugar dispenser was good for a few laughs, and the chicken gravy poured over his meatloaf added a touch of creativity. The chairman was also treated to a stream of complaints about cafeteria facilities, the cafeteria manager, and the company in general (all muttered among the workers as the chairman slid his tray along the serving line). This series of events was followed by (1) an upset stomach, (2) a rise in blood pressure, (3) a heated meeting that afternoon with his executives, and (4) a phone call to my office late that afternoon requesting that I visit the site and make some recommendations.

I was met the following day by an administrative assistant to the vice-president and spent the morning and early part of the afternoon interviewing the cafeteria manager, his supervisor, and several cafeteria workers. I ate lunch in the cafeteria and observed the employees serving their fellow workers cheerfully and efficiently. They could obviously do their job skillfully and well if they wanted.

At 2:00 p.m. I met with the vice-president of human resources. "Well," he said, have you figured out what we can do to fix 'em?" "Fix whom?" I asked. "The cafeteria personnel!" Intrigued, I asked how he thought they might be fixed. "Well, show 'em a movie maybe. You know, something on courtesy, loyalty, and responsibility, and perhaps attitude."

Now I finally understood why they wanted an outside consultant. They wanted the employees "fixed." It never occurred to the chairman or to the vice-president that the management system might be causing the problem.

No, the source of the problem was obviously within the workers, and the company's answer was to hire an individual trained in such things to get the bad attitudes out and put in some good ones. Of course the interviews and analysis conducted indicated a much simpler cause. The workers were being supervised by an Attila the Hun. Coercion was the sole method of influence used. Threats, ridicule, and sarcasm were the order of the day, every day. The employees were not assigned specific responsibilities or given any training. They were a "team," and as such, were expected to pitch in whenever and wherever needed. Performance standards were virtually nonexistent, except to the extent that the cafeteria manager yelled whenever he thought something had not been done properly or quickly enough, and that was often. It would not have been far-fetched to compile a list of performance standards simply by watching to see what had to be done to keep him from yelling!

The simple point to be learned from this incident is that the causes of most performance problems in business can be found in the work environment. It is usually found that management practices, procedures, systems, and company traditions constitute that aspect of the employees' environment that is affecting their performance negatively. Often, the antecedents and consequences of their performance encourage the problem. By changing the environment and managing the consequences properly, managers can create work settings that actually foster good performance. In fact, the most powerful tools available to organizations and managers for affecting performance and changing behavior are the antecedents and consequences they provide each day for specific pinpointed behaviors. Yes, buttons, slogans, and films may bring a smile to the faces of some employees, but chances are they will also bring a frown to the faces of others. There is no empirical evidence that a button, slogan, film, or poster ever reduced errors, decreased the scrap rate, improved response time on service calls, or for that matter, ever increased "job satisfaction," "morale," or "team spirit."

The MBC Decision-Making Process

Building an environment in which good performance flourishes naturally involves making many decisions, as illustrated on page 86.

You have already seen that immediately after pinpointing it must be decided whether the pinpointed behavior is truly performance related. If it is, you proceed with tracking. After using one of the four tracking methods, you again have a decision to make: Is it worth changing this behavior? If you decide that it is, you proceed to an analysis of how the current environment is affecting the pinpointed behavior. This analysis employs two analytical tools that are crucial to MBC: the A-B-C Analysis and B-O-C Audit.

After analyzing properly the set of conditions that is currently affecting the behavior, yet another decision point is reached: Is a change in the environment appropriate or necessary? If the answer is yes, you can proceed with instituting various environmental changes. The decision concerning whether you should make any changes in the first place, as well as the specific changes to institute, will be based on a series of questions you can answer once the analyzing step has been completed. If the answer to the question is "No, a change in the environment is neither necessary nor appropriate," then the MBC approach may not have a further contribution to make.

However, MBC almost always has some contribution to make, even if it is only to indicate that a particular individual needs special medical or psychological help. Not all people can survive in a business or work environment. Some managers find, after going through the MBC decision-making process, that no change in the environment appears necessary, that the current work environment is beneficial for most people most of the time, and that there seems to be no good reason to tamper with it. Their decision at this point would probably be to help the employee get professional help. However, this is the result in only a very small percentage of cases.

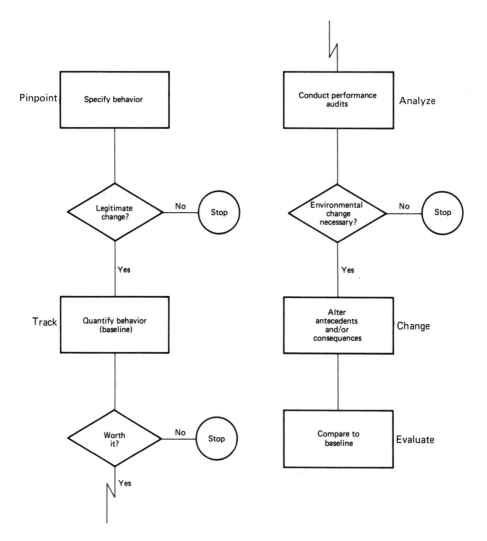

The MBC Decision-Making Process

How to Decide Whether an Environmental Change Is Necessary or Appropriate

The criteria used in MBC to decide whether a change in the environment is necessary and exactly what that change should be are simple and straightforward. First, consider how these criteria are applied in cases involving undesirable behavior, then how they apply to desirable behavior.

The A-B-C Analysis and B-O-C Audit may yield any number of facts that will quickly indicate whether a change is needed and what it should be. These facts are derived from your answers to the series of questions discussed first for undesirable, then desirable behavior.

Deciding How to Change the Environment When You Have Pinpointed an Undesirable Behavior

Does the A-B-C Analysis Show that the Same Antecedent Always Precedes the Undesirable Behavior? One supervisor noted that a particular employee was absent only on days after she had held a "pep talk" to prepare her workers for an anticipated heavy workload. She simply stopped giving the talks, and the employee's attendance improved. (In anticipation of your next question, the supervisor's strategy did not negatively affect the quality of performance of the remaining team members.) If a specific antecedent consistently precedes an undesirable behavior, remove that antecedent and the behavior may stop. An event that precedes a behavior consistently and seems to "get it going" or serve as a "triggering event" for it is called a *prompt*. Removing prompts for undesirable behavior sometimes solves the problem.

Another manager found that *adding* a new prompt provided a solution. In this particular case, an employee had a higher than normal absentee rate on Thursdays, the day that payroll cards had to be posted—a boring, tedious task. It seemed that the prompt for being absent was the fact that "today is Thursday." Obviously, the manager couldn't remove Thursdays from the calendar, so she decided to add a new prompt. On the next Wednesday afternoon, she inquired after the employee's health and made an appointment to help him get started first thing on Thursday morning. She stressed the importance of posting the payroll cards, at the same time acknowledging the drudgery involved. When the employee arrived the following morning, the manager discussed work issues and asked him to call any problems to her attention (an additional new consequence for the employee's improving his Thursday attendance record). This simple strategy solved a long-standing problem.

Does the A-B-C Analysis Fail to Show Any Observable Antecedent that Reliably Precedes the Undesired Behavior? If so, then the people involved may not realize that some aspect of their behavior is indesirable. The solution here is simple: Tell them! Telling an individual something specific about his or her behavior is another form of prompting. Managers' counseling sessions with employees are simply attempts to prompt changes in behavior. The effect of a verbal or written prompt is enhanced when pinpointed behaviors are specified.

Consider the laboratory manager who was called into his boss's office one day. The upper-level manager said, "Dave, have you ever heard of something called maturity?" Confused, Dave answered that naturally he was familiar with the word. "Well, get some!" The meeting was over.

Although Dave certainly didn't go off to look in his local grocery store for a quart of maturity, or to the hardware store for a box of it, that prompt left him feeling confused, upset, and uncertain of how to change or what he was supposed to do differently.

In the discussion of pinpointing, it was shown that this first step, which avoids vague terminology such as labels, sometimes solves problems. However, many managers often progress right through the step of analyzing before they realize that no one has ever really told the employee straight out, in pinpointed terms, that a certain behavior is undesirable. After a workshop in MBC, Dave's boss simply pointed out to him that the jokes, wisecracks, and sarcastic remarks he was making during technical meetings were inappropriate and they were hurting his career. Dave stopped the behavior.

Does the A-B-C Analysis or the B-O-C Audit Show that Reinforcing Consequences Are Following the Undesirable Behavior? So far you have seen numerous examples of managers and organizations making things worse rather than better by inadvertently reinforcing inappropriate or undesired behavior, including the examples of the manager reassuring the complaining programmer, the manager filling out PRFs when employees failed to do so, and the listing of worst offenders. All of these consequences had reinforcing effects on the undesirable behaviors they followed. Again, the solution was simple: Remove the reinforcing consequences for the undesirable behavior. Technically, this procedure is called *extinction*, because one "extinguishes" the undesirable behavior. Further examples of extinction are presented in Chapter 11.

Does the A-B-C Analysis or B-O-C Audit Show that Punishing Consequences Are Following the Undesirable Behavior? If not, then adding a punishing consequence or making the existing punishing consequences more personal, more immediate, or more certain to occur (remember P, I, C?) may solve the problem. Use this approach with caution, however, as you will see when we discuss the management technique of punishing undesirable behavior in Chapter 11.

Now we will turn our attention to the questions you can ask and the decisions you will need to make when the pinpointed behavior of concern to you is a desirable one.

Deciding How to Change the Environment When You Have Pinpointed a Desirable Behavior

In the pinpointing exercise in Chapter 5, you could pinpoint both desirable and undesirable behaviors. You have just seen how the MBC performance-auditing tools can be used to determine whether environmental changes are needed, and what those changes might be when the pinpointed behavior is undesirable. Now think back for a moment to one of the desired behaviors you listed as the questions that follow are pertinent to this category of behavior.

Does the A-B-C Analysis Show that the Same Antecedent Always Precedes the Desirable Behavior? If a particular antecedent or prompt is consistently leading to desirable performance, then ensuring that the antecedent condition occurs regularly usually means that the desirable performance will also occur regularly.

In one pharmaceutical firm, a department head noticed that yields in a certain packaging process varied as much as 35 percent from one day to the next. An A-B-C Analysis indicated that on high-yield days a department supervisor who spent a day in each section was always present in the packaging area. The department head realized that the supervisor's presence was influencing productivity. The supervisor may also have been providing consequences, but this was never observed. The department head then asked the supervisor to reschedule his week so that he visited at least three departments each day and spent no less than 1 hour in any one department. Productivity in all departments increased subsequently and was maintained at the new higher levels.

Does the A-B-C Analysis Fail to Show Any Observable Antecedent that Reliably Precedes the Desired Behavior? If so, one reason the desired behavior is not occurring may be that employees have not been told exactly what is expected of them. Most people want to succeed, and will try very hard to do so. If you tell them what you want them to do, more than likely they will do it. Rules, schedules, timetables, forms, and guidelines are all antecedents or prompts designed to get a behavior going. At times a manager realizes after conducting an A-B-C Analysis that the employee has never been told exactly what to do, or has never seen an example of how a particular job should be done. Adding a new antecedent, in the form of a prompt or model, or using a technique called *shaping*, is often the answer. The change techniques of prompting, modeling, and shaping are discussed in detail in Chapter 9.

In summary, when an A-B-C Analysis indicates that no observable antecedent consistently precedes desired behavior, performance plans, clear-cut objectives, and standards of performance often provide solutions to the problem.

Does the A-B-C Analysis or the B-O-C Audit Show that Reinforcing Consequences Follow the Desired Behavior? If it does, good! At least things are arranged properly. But perhaps you are dissatisfied with the quantity or frequency of the desired behavior. It is possible to make reinforcing consequences more powerful by increasing their size or magnitude, or by making them more personal, more immediate, and more certain to occur.

On the other hand, your analyses and audits sometimes show very few or no reinforcing consequences following the desired behavior. If this is the case, then reinforcing consequences should definitely be introduced.

Does the A-B-C Analysis or B-O-C Audit Show Punishing Consequences Occurring After the Desired Behavior? If punishing consequences are following desired performance, then it is no wonder people are not doing as well as they might. This situation is teaching them not to do just what we would like them to do. (Remember the programmers from Chapter 7 who were criticized after turning in the PRFs?) The obvious step in such a case is to remove the punishing consequences, obstacles, or barriers and then the job will be more likely to get done properly.

In one case, supervisors in a major utility found that estimators were not reporting properly about various aspects of building construction. Their failure to do so was having a negative impact on the productivity of the equipment installers working with them on the job. A lot of time was being wasted when, for example, the installers arrived and found that they had to drill holes and run wires through walls, instead of simply running conduit through dropped ceilings as the estimates had indicated. Why weren't the estimators reporting this critical information? It was discovered that they considered the form used to be lengthy, complex, and "a pain to fill out." What the estimators were really saying was that punishing consequences were involved in doing the job right. The form was simplified and the critical information section modified to a small check-off box on the front page. After those modifications, the installers received accurate information.

The illustration on the opposite page summarizes the process in-

Determining Whether Environmental
Change Is Necessary

(a) When the Pinpointed Behavior Is Undesirable

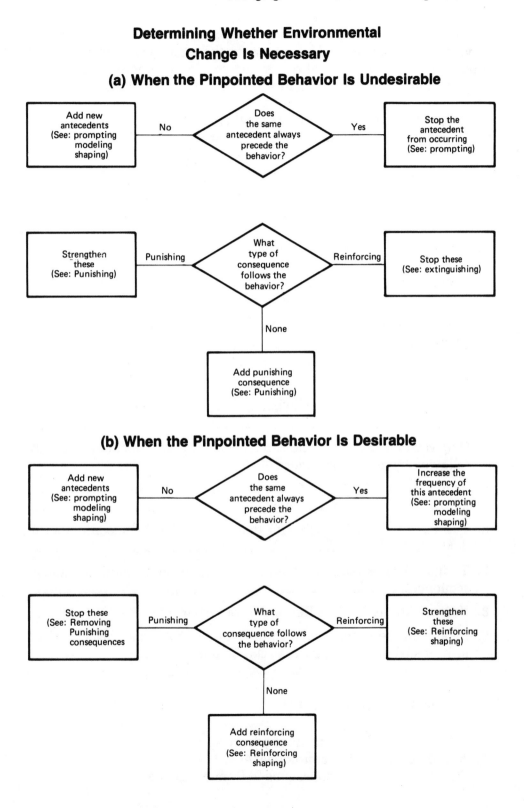

(b) When the Pinpointed Behavior Is Desirable

volved in determining whether or not an environmental change is necessary. It also shows how the answers to the questions just posed lead directly to the development of various change techniques that can be employed to improve performance. These will be discussed in detail in Chapters 9, and 11.

It should now be evident that the MBC approach can be applied to all those areas you learned about in Basic Management 101! Your planning, controlling, organizing, and delegating responsibilities are all affected by what you learn from your analyses of how the environment affects human behavior.

SELF-TEACHING EXERCISE

Complete each of the sentences below using material discussed in this chapter and information shown on page 91.

1. When the same antecedent event always precedes an undesirable behavior, you can change the behavior by _____.

2. If you find a desirable behavior is not systematically followed by any consequence, you can increase the behavior by _____.

3. To change an undesirable behavior that is followed by a reinforcing consequence, _____.

4. One way to decrease an undesired behavior that is not systematically followed by any consequences is to _____.

5. If an A-B-C Analysis or B-O-C Audit shows a punishing consequence following a desirable behavior, _____.

6. To increase desirable behavior that is preceded by specific antecedents, _____.

7. To increase desirable behavior that is followed by reinforcing consequences, _____.

8. You can strengthen a reinforcer or punisher by _____.

9. Details on the specific change procedures that are suggested by the MBC decision-making process can be found _____.

Compare your answers:

1. Stopping the antecedent from occurring
2. Adding a reinforcing consequence
3. Stop the reinforcing consequence from occurring

4. Add punishing consequences
5. The punishing consequence should be removed
6. Increase the frequency of the antecedent
7. Strengthen the reinforcing consequences
8. Making it more personal, immediate, and certain to occur, and also by increasing its size
9. In Chapters 9, 10 and 11

CHAPTER NINE
CHANGING ANTECEDENTS

If you have been following the suggested steps in the Management by Consequences decision-making process for a behavior you would like to change, you have now reached the point where you must decide what specific change technique or procedure would be most likely to produce a change in behavior. We are not thinking here, of course, about changing an individual's attitudes, motivations, drives, or needs. Effective managers understand that people motivate themselves. What you can do, however, as a manager, and are in fact responsible for, is create an environment in which most people choose most often to act productively. People who choose to engage in productive behavior are usually referred to as "motivated" or even "highly motivated." This is not to say, however, that people who behave nonproductively are not motivated. Unfortunately, their motivation is to thwart organizational goals, or at least to behave in ways that fail to support them.

The effective change procedures used by managers are consistent with the science of human behavior discussed in earlier chapters and are based on the principles of human learning, reinforcement, and operant conditioning. Most of these effective procedures can be categorized into one of the eight change techniques illustrated in Table 7.

A-B-C Analyses and B-O-C Audits will suggest the specific change techniques or combination of techniques that are likely to be the most effective in improving performance.

Changing Antecedents to Change Behavior

Prompting

Prompting is simply anything you do to get a behavior going. It is an antecedent event, an event that occurs before a behavior and that is designed to influence the quantity and form of the behavior. Rules,

---

TABLE 7 **The Eight MBC Change Techniques**

Tools for Changing Antecedents:
  Prompting
  Modeling
Tools for Changing Consequences:
  Reinforcing
  Removing punishers
  Extinguishing
  Reinforcing opposite behavior
  Punishing
  Shaping

---

schedules, lists of things to do, handbooks, training programs, signs, verbal requests, commands, and yellow lines on the floor of a warehouse designed to guide towmotor operators are all forms of prompts. Most managers and supervisors know about prompts, yet it is amazing how often the solution to a performance problem is to enhance the quality of prompts.

For example, during an MBC workshop a group of managers and executives were asked to identify their most serious concerns regarding employee performance. A manager of two shifts of security officers began by saying he had a group of employees who were "lazy, unmotivated, had a bad attitude, and just didn't care." (He had not yet learned to pinpoint.) After training in pinpointing, the manager revised his statement as follows: "My people are not responding to 'hot' items." He then further defined "hot items" for the workshop participants.

One hot item involved a visit to the site by a division vice-president. The vice-president had flown into the small local airport from corporate headquarters, where he was to be picked up by car and driven to the site. It was the responsibility of the manager's personnel to arrange for the car. They did not. Therefore, the vice-president stood in the cold at the airport for over 45 minutes with the wind whipping around his ankles. This was certainly a hot item! Other hot items involved such performance deficits as failure to lock or unlock doors when the employee badge system for entering secure areas was inoperative because of on-site construction. In general, it was found that the items not being handled properly involved changes in daily activities that required responses from the security officers.

After pinpointing the problem, the manager said it would be easy enough to track simply by counting the number of hot items that came up each week and comparing the total to the number that had been handled appropriately. He estimated that in any one week there might be six to twelve hot items, whereas the number of failures to respond was probably between one and four. However, even one failure to respond was unsatisfactory.

Using the A-B-C Analysis, the manager then *analyzed* the antecedents and consequences of "responding to hot items." As he did so, he began to realize that it was difficult for the employees to differentiate between "hot items" and "not-so-hot items." At the site location was a bulletin board covered with 8½ × 11 inch size white sheets of paper, in addition to a clipboard each employee was supposed to check. Some sheets were 6 months old, others were newly posted. Even though the employees were expected to check the bulletin board and clipboard daily, they were somehow missing the hot items. The manager therefore decided to make them easier to identify. To this end, he instructed his secretary to place a red sticker in the lower right-hand corner of the hot item sheets only. He determined each day what tasks were hot items. In addition, he had a rubber stamp made with several blank lines on it so employees could initial the hot items after reading them. These new prompts helped personnel identify hot items. In addition, the manager systematically spoke to each employee who initialed the sheets to express his appreciation, arranging his schedule over a 3-week period so that he came in early for one shift or stayed late to meet another. He made comments like, "Thanks, I notice you're initialing the hot items. It helps me to know you're aware of them." This expression of appreciation, a consequence for initialing the sheets, was designed to encourage the initialing.

Within 8 weeks the manager reported that the problem was solved. All hot items were being handled in a timely manner. The manager's original opinion that the employees had a "bad attitude, lacked motivation, were lazy, and didn't care" had changed. He realized that a change in the environment was all that was really necessary to help them perform better. The new words and procedures made the difference.

Prompting is a simple technique, but it can often solve a problem. Prompting is more likely to be effective if we also build in reinforcing consequences to support the new behavior once it has occurred. Counseling and coaching sessions are prompts that managers often use to get employees to change some behavior. The quality of a counseling session can be improved if the words managers use include pinpointed behaviors.

Modeling

Effective managers understand that one of their most powerful tools for influencing the behavior of others is the example they themselves set.

One supervisor pinpointed as a concern the behavior of "complaining." He said his employees were constantly moaning and groaning about company policies, the temperature of the offices, their workspace, their equipment, and almost anything else one could imagine. Yet at lunch that day in the company cafeteria, this same supervisor was heard to remark, "The only place I know that can ruin a grilled cheese sandwich;" "I knew I should have brought my parka! What's the temperature in here anyway?" "These tables are cleaned once a month, whether they need it or not!" Perhaps this inadvertent modeling of an inappropriate behavior had much to do with the manager's own "complaining" problem!

Managers sometimes pinpoint the problem of senior staff personnel not doing complete work. They indicate that their people's reports often lack depth or quality, as measured by the number of recommendations that are made without proper documentation or supporting evidence; that reports may be submitted late or contain errors; or that they may contain a great many facts, but lack syntheses of these facts or even final recommendations. An A-B-C Analysis often helps the manager to see that the employee has never, in fact, been shown an example of a high-quality report. Providing employees with good models at the outset often prevents problems from occurring. When managers complain about the time involved in giving detailed instructions (prompts) and good examples (models), they should keep in mind the old adage about never having enough time to do it right, but always having enough time to do it over.

In instances where employees do not perform adequately when making public presentations, it is often because they have never seen one given effectively. Just as it is a sound instructional method to have sales trainees observe models of superior sales representatives making calls, the same type of training can be used to increase employee effectiveness in-house.

An instructor responsible for teaching table service skills at a prestigious culinary training school produced significant improvements in student performance as well as reductions in training time when he instituted the procedure of having his students eat dinner at a fine restaurant. He explained, "I was expecting 18-year-olds to know how to provide first-class restaurant service when the only model of service most of them had seen was at the local fast food restaurant."

It is interesting in the world of work to notice the number of times that managers, supervisors, and directors criticize employees for doing the same things they themselves do.

A college dean complained that department chairpersons were always late in meeting deadlines, which meant that he regularly had to assign his secretary the task of telephoning tardy chairpersons each time a report or some paperwork was overdue. Yet when the chairpersons were interviewed, one of their strongest criticisms of the dean's performance was that he rarely met his commitments and was "always" late with promised answers to questions, decisions, or actions. If this was really the case, then he was certainly not setting an appropriate model for his chairpersons.

An executive responsible for a planning group explained that one of the worst things a product planner could do was tell engineers how to build a product. Planners are responsible for determining consumer needs and for specifying product function. Once the functions are specified, the engineers are responsible for building a product to meet those functions. Some planners, however, tend to get too technically involved and try to tell the engineers how to design products. Not only is this resented by the engineers, but it often delays the project and usually results in poorer engineering designs. Nevertheless, the very executive who made this comment was himself well known for trying to stipulate to engineers exactly what metals should be used in a particular product, how the power supplies should be mounted, how they should be ventilated, and so on. With this behavior being modeled by the top executive, it was no wonder that so many employees who reported to him were doing the same thing.

Such behaviors as keeping one's desk and office in order, being courteous on the telephone, or dressing in a businesslike fashion are also behaviors that can be powerfully influenced by simply setting the appropriate model. It is nothing less than hypocrisy when top management demands, expects, or requires certain patterns of behavior from subordinates and then fails to model these behaviors themselves.

In many companies, booklets, manuals, memos, and meetings are used to stress the importance of performance appraisal programs. Despite this, many employees are not told clearly what is expected of them or how well they are doing. A company which finds that a large percentage of its managers are not conducting employee performance appraisals properly will invariably also find that the managers themselves are not receiving appraisals from the people to whom they report.

The procedure of modeling demonstrates clearly that the "Do as I say, not as I do" approach is counterproductive in business. Prompting and modeling are both procedures that involve antecedent changes. Of course, if employees are already doing something, or start to do something, and then see top management modeling the behavior, the modeling may encourage the employees to continue what they are doing. In this case the behavior of top management may also be serving as a reinforcing consequence.

In one manufacturing firm, executives and managers used signs to prompt the wearing of safety glasses; they also agreed to model this behavior. Over a 2-month period the number of employees wearing safety glasses on the workfloor increased significantly. When interviewed, the employees wearing glasses made such comments as "When I see an executive wearing glasses, I know they must think it's important." Or "You get the feeling the glasses are for everyone, so I don't mind wearing them." Or "It's kind of become the 'in thing' to do."

Antecedent changes, such as prompting and modeling, are powerful. Managers sensitive to the tremendous impact the environment has on behavior will often look to the quality of their own instructions, examples, training programs, or performance plans when trying to troubleshoot performance problems. Less effective managers assume the problem lies within the employee.

Prompting and modeling are both examples of antecedent changes that can lead to improved performance. However, sometimes an A-B-C Analysis shows that current antecedents are adequate or that it may not be possible to alter them. In such cases you can consider the six types of changes in consequences that are part of the Management by Consequences approach.

Please note that the Self-Teaching exercises for Chapters 9, 10, and 11 all appear at the end of Chapter 11 since the eight tools you will need to complete the exercises are taught in these three chapters.

CHAPTER TEN
CHANGING CONSEQUENCES TO INCREASE APPROPRIATE BEHAVIOR

Changing Consequences to Change Behavior

Reinforcing Productive Behavior

It should be recalled that reinforcement is the process by which certain consequences strengthen the behavior they follow. You also know that reinforcers can inadvertently strengthen inappropriate behavior. This is illustrated in the cartoon below.

Adults can also get caught up in the misuse of reinforcement, as illustrated on page 102.

Effective managers and leaders not only know how to avoid this trap, but are also able to use reinforcers systematically to strengthen productive behavior. Successful managers know that it is "good business" to maintain and encourage effective behaviors that result in quality products.

Three classes of events can be used to reinforce desired behavior in organizations:

An Example of How Reinforcers Can Inadvertently Strengthen Inappropriate Behavior

An Example of the Misuse of Reinforcement
Reprinted by permission of the Chicago Tribune–New York News Syndicate, Inc.

- *Social reinforcers* are people-to-people kinds of events. A smile, a word of thanks, and a pat on the back are examples of social reinforcers.
- *Activity reinforcers* are preferred tasks or prestigious assignments that can be awarded following an achievement to reinforce that achievement.
- *Tangible reinforcers* are such things as money, awards, and gifts that can be provided contingent upon good performance.

Table 8 lists some items that have worked as reinforcers in a wide variety of organizations.

You will notice some overlapping in the categories. A dinner paid for by the company has a social component (it is shared with other people), an activity component (it is a preferred activity), and a tangible component (a check or voucher). An employee does not say, "Well, let's see. My boss has given me two social reinforcers and a tangible; I guess I'm due for an activity." These categories are used simply to suggest the wide variety of options available to an organization for reinforcing appropriate performance.

You may be thinking at this point that the concept of reinforcement is nothing new, that companies have been doing this kind of thing for years. It is true that award programs and incentive plans have existed for

---

TABLE 8 **Some Items that Serve as Reinforcers**

Social:	Tangible:
Verbal or nonverbal recognition or compliments	Desk accessories
	Wall plaques
Letter of appreciation	Company car
Feedback on performance	Watches
Invitations to have coffee or lunch	Trophies
Solicitations for suggestions	Commendations
Solicitations for advice	Rings/tie pins
Compliments on work progress	Appliances and furniture for the home
Recognition in company publications	Clothing/uniforms
Pat on the back	Office with a window
Smile	Redecoration of work environment
	Company literature
Activity:	Private office
Job with more responsibility	Coffee break treats
Job rotation	Bonuses
Early time off with pay	Stocks
Extended breaks	Stock options
Extended lunch period	Movie passes
Personal time off with pay	Trading stamps (green stamps)
Working on personal project on company time	Paid-up insurance policies
	Dinner theatre tickets
Use of company machinery or facilities for personal projects	Vacation trips
	Coupons redeemable at local stores
Taking over for manager when the manager is off site	Coupons for free coffee during breaks
Popular speakers or lectures	
Opportunity to make a presentation at a meeting	
Special assignments	
Dinners for the family on the company	
Opportunity to attend a conference or seminar	

a long time. What is surprising, however, is how often they are used unscientifically or inefficiently.

Often, the pinpointed behaviors required to earn a reward are unclear. A company may provide awards for pinpointed behaviors that do not lead to desired end results. For example, one manufacturing firm held a contest involving a cash award for the employee who produced the largest number of screwdrivers. It was discovered later that, in an attempt to break the record, the winner often skipped the process that ensured a tight bond between the plastic handle and the metal part of the tool. So, although the employee produced the most screwdrivers, he also produced the largest number of defective ones. It is therefore important to reinforce quality as well as quantity.

The concept of reinforcement is not new, but the systematic, scientific use of reinforcement to increase productivity and quality is sorely lacking in most organizations. Effective managers take advantage of the wide variety of reinforcers available. They do not rely solely on tangible reinforcers, but are creative in their use of social and activity reinforcers as well. Some managers do restrict themselves to the use of tangible reinforcers, such as awards programs, contests, and incentive plans. The trouble then is that when managers most need them in times of business downturn or strong competition, they often can least afford them. However, social reinforcers cost nothing, and neither do activity reinforcers. These powerful tools for change are often overlooked by less effective managers.

Some managers and supervisors say it is not their style to compliment or reinforce individuals. That response, however, is akin to a doctor saying it is not his or her style to use antiseptic on a wound. Managers cannot avoid influencing people. If they are not using reinforcement, they will probably be using punishment, and punishment can have serious side effects and complications, as discussed in Chapter 11.

However, the question of style is important. Many effective leaders are not highly verbal but show by their actions that they know how to use reinforcement. Giving attention and recognition to others is a powerful type of reinforcement. Attention is such a powerful reinforcer that, if you withhold your attention for good performance and only attend to poor performance, you may inadvertently reinforce the poor performance, as shown in previous examples. If a manager does not build a track record of responding to achievements, then it is likely that the attention paid to poor performance may backfire.

Why is it that managers and organizations seem to pay so much attention to poor performance and often ignore good performance? The reason may be that those promoted or appointed to supervisory positions have a long history of being reinforced for error detection and problem solving. Most managers are promoted for their technical ability, not necessarily for their people-management skills. When they take on people-management responsibilities, they may tend to practice the same techniques with people that worked with machines. Think about it. You don't often see an engineer or programmer patting a computer on the back and saying, "Well done, you haven't dropped any data today." A machine that is working is left alone. If it breaks down, you turn your attention to the problem and fix it.

Error detection is a way of life for most people in business and industry. This strong reliance on error detection skills may carry over when working with people. But people need more than just feedback on their errors. People work best when they get balanced feedback on what they do well as well as what they do poorly. Managers who say it is not their "style" to give positive feedback are denying their people something they need to perform well.

When you think about it, technically oriented people also do more with machines than simply detect errors. It is usually cost effective to practice preventive maintenance with machines and equipment. Paying attention to machinery when it is working well and taking some time to oil the moving parts and remove any dust and dirt can lengthen machine life and protect your investment. People are the most costly investment in any business, so you might well ask yourself what preventive maintenance you are practicing with people. What are you doing to assure that they keep performing well? One thing you might do that is analogous to preventive maintenance with machines is to reinforce appropriate behavior consciously and systematically. When you reinforce systematically, you are practicing *achievement detection*.

How do you carry out achievement detection? Most current error detection systems usually turn out to be excellent achievement detection systems as well. A 3 percent "scrap rate" is also a 97 percent "appropriate utilization of materials." The employee complaint that "No one here ever tells you when you do something right. You only hear from management when you make a mistake" is often a legitimate one.

One company found that achievement detection could be very important in saving money in the accounts payable area. This firm uses a number called the "lost discount rate" to measure losses incurred when its bills are not paid on time. On orders for millions of dollars worth of raw material, the ½ percent or 1 percent discount that many vendors grant for quick payment can amount to a considerable sum. It was the practice of the home office to audit various operating units to determine their lost discount rate. These audits took place at various times. But some managers chose to "accentuate the positive" and reinforce appropriate behavior in their teams. These managers asked each employee in their departments to keep a running list of "attained discounts," the dollar amount saved when payment was processed in a timely manner. These managers held weekly meetings to discuss the department's weekly attained discount and what each employee had done to contribute to the saving. The list of attained discounts and weekly meetings were more personal, immediate, and certain consequences than the random audits conducted by the home office, which were perceived as other, delayed, and uncertain.

The bottom-line results showed that the departments with managers who chose to reinforce appropriate behavior did significantly better than other departments whose managers did not seek to reinforce achievements.

Achievement detection is simple, often costs nothing, and yet can yield significant benefits.

The Compliment:Criticism Ratio

One way to check your personal use of reinforcement is to audit your own compliment:criticism ratio. Compliments on good performance, praise, and positive feedback often serve as reinforcers. But of course praise is not reinforcing to everyone. Some employees value only monetary reinforcement, so when a supervisor says, "Well done," they reply, "Yeah, just put it in my paycheck." For such individuals praise or compliments are not reinforcers, and supervisors soon learn this.

But assuming that compliments and other forms of positive feedback are reinforcing for many people, you can check your compliment:criticism ratio to get an idea of how effectively you are taking advantage of reinforcement principles.

Each day you engage in certain activities. You write memos, talk to individuals, make phone calls, hold one-on-one sessions, and participate in meetings. What if you kept a 3×5 inch size card in your pocket or on your desk and simply put a plus sign (+) on one side of the card each time you attempt to reinforce someone by giving that individual positive feedback. On the other side of the card put a minus sign (−) each time you criticize or give negative feedback in an attempt to decrease some behavior or action. What would your ratio of compliments to criticism look like at the end of a week or month? If you are satisfied with your relationship with other team members or employees, then this number may represent part of the reason for your success. In such cases there would be no need to change it. However, if you are not satisfied with your ability to influence others, you might try to alter this ratio. Usually you will find that the critical remarks outnumber the compliments. Try accentuating more positive things that people do. This does not mean condoning or ignoring poor performance, just trying to achieve a better balance.

Some effective leaders make more positive statements than negative ones. They say this is easy because most of the time people are doing well. They further report that by building on strengths, it is easier when they do have to give negative feedback because they have established a good record of responding to and recognizing achievements. The verbal report that employees often make about managers who have a balanced compliment:criticism ratio is "my boss is fair" or "she's tough, but fair." This appears to be recognition by employees that their boss knows their strengths as well as their weaknesses.

Reinforcement need not be verbal, as shown by the list in Table 8. Many effective leaders are not highly verbal, as mentioned earlier. But they do use other, nonverbal means of positive feedback and are also skillful in using activities and tangible reinforcers. The compliment:criticism ratio is simply a technique of self-assessment. Keep in mind that what you intend as a compliment may be perceived by someone else as a put-down. If in doubt, you might ask others such simple questions as:

• "Are there some things I say or do that turn you off or make you upset?"

or

• "What are the things I say that let you know I think you're doing well?"

Such questions provide feedback from others on the words and procedures you can use to communicate effectively. If you have never asked this kind of question, you may feel uncomfortable at first, but the information you obtain may make a big difference in your future behavior.

No set or rigid number for the compliment:criticism ratio works all the time. Some managers are successful with a fairly even balance. On the other hand, many managers' and supervisors' compliments outweigh their criticisms by 2:1 or even 4:1. They are not "giving the shop away." What they are doing is systematically trying to increase appropriate behavior and eliminate inappropriate behavior. The ratio will vary depending on the situation, but at least these managers are aware of the powerful impact their words can have on others. To these managers "discipline" means "training," and good training involves more than just negative feedback.

A Word About Sincerity

When dealing with compliments and praise, people often ask such questions as:

• "Isn't sincerity important?"
• "Will I be sincere if I try for some artificial ratio?"
• "Can you praise so much that it loses its effectiveness?"
• "Won't people become too dependent on compliments?"
• "Can too much reinforcement hurt people?"

Of course, sincerity is important. Supervisors should not say "well done" if they do not feel the praise is deserved. But the problem is usually not that people are undeserving of compliments, but that supervisors are too busy or unaware of the need to give recognition.

A more basic issue has to do with the way our society reacts to reinforcement and punishment in general. The set of questions just listed is legitimate and fair, but another set of questions that *should* be asked seldom is:

• "Isn't sincerity important when we criticize people?"
• "Can you criticize so much that it loses its effectiveness?"
• "Won't people become too dependent on criticism?"
• "Could my use of fear tactics hurt my employees?"

Few doubt the sincerity of criticism or negative feedback. Few seem to worry about the use of punitive control in organizations. Yet when punishment is used to change behavior, it can result in at least five serious complications or negative side effects.

The point is simply that managers must be careful with whatever techniques they use to influence the behavior of others. They can overdo it with their attempts to use either reinforcement or punishment. A balanced approach where the consequences fit the performance is what makes a supervisor, manager, or leader most effective. And in terms of sincerity, because few ever doubt that criticism is sincere, if the same skills and timing are used with compliments, then they will probably be perceived as being sincere as well.

Some Suggestions for Using Reinforcers

Some simple guidelines for using reinforcement will help you to achieve maximum effectiveness in your work environment.

Guideline 1: Reinforcers Should Be Given *After* the Desired Behavior Occurs

Some managers have told me that they tried to use reinforcement, but it did not work. One supervisor reported:

"I tried to reinforce her. I told her that she could take Friday off, but that she had to promise to get through our backlog of orders on Monday, even if it meant working overtime. She took Friday off all right, but she was late getting in on Monday and had to leave at 5:00 p.m. because her ride home left then and her car was in the shop. So the backlog never did get processed that day."

The supervisor tried to influence his employee by providing a desired event—taking the day off—prior to the desired performance. This technique rarely works well. What he did reinforce was the employee's behavior of asking for a day off and promising to get through the backlog. Reinforcement should always *follow* desired performance.

Guideline 2: Reinforcers Should Be Provided as Soon as Possible After the Desired Behavior

Other things being equal, the more immediate the reinforcement, the more powerful it is in terms of strengthening behavior. This is why a smile, a word of thanks, a brief conversation over a cup of coffee are all more powerful than a gold watch at the end of 25 years of "meritorious service." Skilled managers are vigilant in looking for achievements to recognize and reinforce. They get a lot of mileage out of the small things they do because they know the value of immediate reinforcers. Of course, formal recognition programs often have built-in delays. It takes time to make justifications and get approvals. Savvy managers use their own words of appreciation and other social reinforcers to bridge the gap between the completion of some task and the delivery of larger, more tangible reinforcers.

Guideline 3: Reinforcers Should Be Personal in Impact

This does not mean you cannot reinforce teamwork, but that each member of the team should perceive the consequence provided as truly reinforcing.

An executive for an east coast firm arranged for a trip to San Francisco for his department heads and their spouses to recognize and reinforce the team for meeting all sales targets during the last fiscal year. Over half the people involved said they appreciated the thought, but wished he had asked them first:

• "He likes San Francisco, but I go there three times a month on business."
• "My husband and I would have preferred a week at Dartmouth College; they're having a great lecture series this summer."

Strong leaders take time to find out what is reinforcing to each individual. They don't assume they know; they ask. In one company a middle manager called the wife of one of his employees and found out that the employee had always wanted to build a grandfather clock. The employee was extremely touched when the kit was presented at an informal breakfast meeting. That manager knew the value of personalizing reinforcers.

Guideline 4: Reinforcers Should Be Delivered Consistently

You are probably familiar with the problem of unfair, inconsistent reward systems: "Over there, if you come in to work on time they give you a bonus. Here you have to walk on water to get a smile."

Less effective managers and organizations either fail to get the full benefit from reinforcers or, worse yet, may actually destroy morale and productivity through their inept use of reinforcement. Employees have a right to know the rules. If rules change (and they must from time to time), they have a right to know about the changes. Some managers seem to like to play the game of "hot and cold" with their employees:

> "I won't tell you what I expect or what my rules for delivering reinforcement are. You just keep trying random behaviors, and I'll smile (or give an award, and so on) if you get it right. I'll frown (or scream, yell, threaten, or withhold rewards) if you get it wrong. Now, don't assume that the rules are the same for you as they are for Harry (who's doing the same job as you). You see, Harry and I go back a long way. Oh, and don't assume the rules will be the same for you tomorrow as they are today. See, we like to keep you guessing here. It promotes flexibility, creativity, and good stuff like that."

Simply put, what are the rules for delivering reinforcers and punishers in your organization? The exercise of discussing the pinpointed behaviors openly and honestly and the end results valued that will lead to recognition can be a powerful exercise. Many effective managers and supervisors hold such discussions with their employees and find the sessions worthwhile. But it is important to keep pinpointing. It is not sufficient to say, "We reinforce loyalty, hard work, caring, and cooperation." Give examples. What pinpointed behaviors constitute being loyal and working hard? What can they say and do that will show they care and that will demonstrate cooperation? Answers to crucial questions can help you be more consistent in your delivery of reinforcers.

In summary, reinforcement is one of the most powerful but least-used tools in the world of work. Experienced, successful people know the value of "walking softly and carrying a big reinforcer."

Removing Punishing Consequences

Another method of changing consequences to change behavior is to remove those consequences that are currently punishing the desired behavior. Remember the programmers who were asked to fill out the program report forms (PRFs)? Consider the A-B-C Analysis in below.

Antecedent	Behavior	Consequence
Programmers are asked to fill out PRFs.	A programmer fills out a PRF.	The manager criticizes the programmer based on information included in the PRF.

There is no mystery as to why the programmers tended not to fill out the PRFs. A simple change procedure would be to stop criticizing the programmers after they filled them out. Far too frequently managers inadvertently punish the very behavior they would like to increase:

> "That's great, Hal, your report is in on time. Maybe we should have it framed and put on display. A timely report from you is certainly a rarity!"

Sarcastic remarks often backfire. Productive organizations will not allow good behavior to be punished. They are open enough to analyze their own practices, procedures, policies, and traditions to make sure they are not punishing good performance.

In a company that managed a chain of franchised hotels and motels, one executive responsible for housekeeping complained about the "lackadaisical attitude" of many maids:

> "They just do the bare minimum to get by. Tell them you want four rooms an hour, and that's what you get. They don't strive for excellence."

Putting aside the fact that it's hard to "strive for excellence" while you're trying to eke out a living on minimum wage, consider what an A-B-C Analysis yielded.

Antecedent	Behavior	Consequence
A maid is asked to get done with her assigned rooms as soon as possible because there are many early check-ins.	The maid exceeds this goal and finishes well ahead of time.	The maid is asked to move to another floor and help out a person who is "slow as molasses."

Some may feel that employees should not be affected by such consequences. They feel employees should "pitch in" and "pick up the slack" created by those who are less productive. Many people will do this—at least for a while. But if management continues to reinforce inappropriate performance on the part of some and allows punishing consequences to follow the good performance of others, this will result in a classic "unhealthy organization," and unhealthy organizations find it tough to make a profit because so much employee time is spent in unproductive behavior.

Before labeling people who are not performing up to standard as "lazy," "unmotivated," or as having "a bad attitude," try an A-B-C Analysis or a Balance of Consequences Audit. Interview employees. Ask them what they perceive the consequences or "payoffs" to be for doing certain tasks. You may be surprised to find that desirable behavior is being punished. But that is far better than trying to deal with "laziness," "motivation," or "attitudes." You don't know how to change those things. You do know, however, that a change in management practices, procedures, company policy, or company tradition will remove punishing consequences—and this is often the solution.

Please note that the self-teaching exercises for Chapters 9, 10, and 11 all appear at the end of Chapter 11 since the eight tools you will need to complete the exercises are taught in these three chapters.

CHAPTER ELEVEN
DECREASING INAPPROPRIATE BEHAVIOR AND ENCOURAGING NEW BEHAVIOR

Extinguishing Inappropriate Behavior

Extinguishing refers to the procedure of preventing reinforcing consequences from following any behavior you would like to see decrease. Just as fire needs oxygen, heat, and combustible material, human behavior needs reinforcement and a person to engage in the behavior. If you remove the reinforcement (for example, stop laughing politely at a comedian's bad jokes) or remove the person from the reinforcing environment (use a long pole with a hook on the end to yank the comedian off the stage), the poor performance will stop. You don't have to punish the comedian (throw tomatoes, or boo and hiss). All you have to do is extinguish the behavior by withholding reinforcement.

One executive tells of a staff member who would tell old war stories, ramble on during conversations, get involved in long, drawn-out explanations, and "beat around the bush" before getting down to business. The executive wanted the staff member to "net things out," cite specific facts, and make crisp, short, statements. He had discussed the problem with the staff member at least twice, and even though the employee agreed it was a problem, the "rambling" behavior did not decrease.

An A-B-C Analysis yielded some interesting information, as shown below.

Antecedent	Behavior	Consequence
A conversation occurs between a staff member and an executive.	The staff member "rambles."	The executive nods his head in agreement, smiles politely, and asks questions about the rambling content.

A-B-C Analysis of Staff Member's Behavior

In an attempt to "be polite," "show interest," and "show respect," the executive was providing a consequence that reinforced the very behavior both parties agreed was a problem and wanted to decrease.

A B-O-C Audit yielded additional useful information, as shown below.

The executive could see that he was creating an unhealthy situation with respect to the staff member's behavior. Whenever the staff member provided factual information, the executive stood up and ended the meeting. This abrupt withdrawal of attention may have been punishing or discouraging crisp conversation. The punishing consequences outweighed the reinforcing consequences for the desired behavior. In addition, the reinforcing consequences outweighed the punishing consequences for the undesired behavior. The executive decided to alter the consequences by systematically changing his own behavior to see if this would influence the behavior of the staff member. His action plan is shown on page 115.

As can be seen from the figure, the executive rearranged the consequences so that no reinforcement followed the undesired behavior. His action plan moved the reinforcing consequences so that they followed

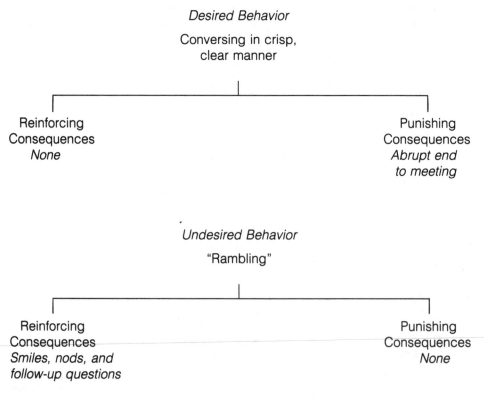

Desired Behavior

Conversing in crisp,
clear manner

Reinforcing
Consequences
None

Punishing
Consequences
*Abrupt end
to meeting*

Undesired Behavior

"Rambling"

Reinforcing
Consequences
*Smiles, nods, and
follow-up questions*

Punishing
Consequences
None

Audit of Staff Member's Conversational Behavior

Desired Behavior

Conversing in crisp,
clear manner

Reinforcing
Consequences
1. *Smile, nod,*
   express interest;
   use follow-up
   questions
2. *Comment on how*
   helpful crisp
   recommendations are

Punishing
Consequences
None

Undesired Behavior

"Rambling"

Reinforcing
Consequences
None
(Stop previous action)

Punishing
Consequences
None

B-O-C Audit Showing Changes Made by Executive

the desired behavior. This is actually a combination of "extinction" of the undesired behavior and reinforcement of the desired behavior. After making these changes the executive reported that the problem was solved within three meetings.

In Chapter 1 you saw another example of extinction when a manager helped a programmer to stop complaining so much. The manager removed the reinforcing consequences for complaining, at the same time reinforcing problem-solving behavior. In most cases extinction of an undesired behavior should be coupled with reinforcement of a desired behavior. If this is not done, the decrease in the undesired behavior will result in a temporary "behavioral vacuum" into which other behavior will flow. The other behavior that fills the vacuum may be another undesired or inappropriate one (Murphy's Law being what it is, this is usually the case!). A skillful manager designs an environment to ensure that useful behavior fills the vacuum. This environmental design involves altering antecedents and consequences.

Extinction should not be construed as condoning or ignoring inappropriate behavior. A manager using MBC who has taken the trouble to pinpoint, track, analyze, change, and evaluate is certainly not ignoring or condoning poor performance. The manager is, however, using techniques other than yelling, screaming, and threatening; the results in terms of actual, long-lasting behavior change prove this is a superior management method.

A Word of Caution: Extinction Takes Time

One manager tried the technique of extinction when a marketing representative who reported to him told "crude, childish" jokes in the office. Prior to using extinction, she had casually mentioned that the jokes were "kind of off-color," but because she did not want to hurt the long-term employee's feelings she had not pressed the issue.

The manager went on to conduct an A-B-C Analysis and realized that, in an attempt to be polite when the employee cracked a joke, and also partly out of personal embarrassment, she would typically smile and say something like, "Bill, you're always coming up with these jokes; you've got a million of them." She concluded that this consequence might be reinforcing the bad jokes, so decided not to smile, but instead to look down during the telling of the joke and not to make any remark after the punch line.

About 2 weeks after the manager began implementing her plan, however, the employee was telling more jokes, and they were getting raunchier. This sometimes happens. Extinction takes time, and things may get worse before they get better. Think of it: When you use a pay telephone or a coin-operated dispensing machine and it doesn't work, you don't get the reinforcement you expected. What do you do? You may bang, pound, or kick it, You try harder. When a long history of receiving reinforcement for a particular behavior is suddenly stopped (extinction is used), for a time most people try a little harder. They act as if the coin is stuck. And this is precisely what the marketing rep did—he tried harder. He spoke louder and told raunchier jokes. But ultimately he gave up. Before too long the employee had "finally gotten the message." The jokes stopped and more productive conversation replaced it, which the manager was quick to reinforce. Remember, extinction may take a little longer, but the long-term results are usually well worth it.

In summary, whenever an A-B-C Analysis or B-O-C Audit show that reinforcers are following undesired behavior, a useful procedure is to stop those reinforcers from occurring. That is what extinction is all about.

Reinforcing Opposite Behavior

Far too often when managers identify a behavior they would like to see stop or diminish in frequency, they think punishment is the only way to influence that behavior. Our society—our schools, homes, and places of business display all sorts of rules along with the dire, punishing consequences for failure to comply with them.

Accentuating the positive is at the heart of the MBC approach. Not only does this approach advocate reinforcement rather than punishment, it also advocates focusing on what is wanted rather than what isn't. Think of it. Dozens (hundreds? thousands?) of behaviors can interfere with achieving the objectives and goals of a business or business project. But relatively few key behaviors contribute to the needs of the business. Effective managers save much time and effort by focusing on these vital few positive, desirable behaviors, rather than trying to punish the many trivial, nonproductive behaviors that could absorb their time. This is not to say that they do not know how to use punishment (you will see what this punishment involves later in this chapter), but it does say that because they design the work environment so well, the amount of time spent on punishment is relatively small.

The key to reinforcing opposite behavior is to ask the following question when confronted with an undesirable behavior you would like to see decrease or stop: "What alternate behavior would I like to see occurring that would be incompatible with or opposite to the undesired behavior?" The answer to this question will usually indicate what behaviors you should reinforce. Then simply put to use the techniques outlined to reinforce productive behavior. An example of reinforcing opposite behavior was seen in the section on extinguishing, when the executive reinforced concise conversation at the same time he was extinguishing rambling.

In one company, a new, young first-line manager took over a manufacturing engineering department that included an older, long-term employee who had been labeled an "attitude problem" and "possible troublemaker" for the past 5 or 6 years. The employee had a high absenteeism and lateness record. He was frequently sent to the medical department, but always returned with reports that no medical condition could be identified that would interfere with his ability to do the job or report to work regularly and on time.

The manager reviewed this employee's personnel file and found that he had had at least three other managers over the last 6 years. All had indicated that this was a "problem employee." The new manager asked himself, "What new, wonderful, earth-shattering thing can I do that has not already been done by my predecessors? They have tried it all, threats, embarrassment, harrassment, ridicule, cajoling, reasoning." The only thing that occurred to him was that maybe this employee would like to retire with a little dignity. There had been a preponderance of punishment over the years. No wonder he preferred to stay home. The manager decided to try reinforcing opposite behavior. The employee was technically competent and knew his job well, so the manager decided to let him know that he appreciated his knowledge and skills and gave him a part of the work he could call his own. The manager's predecessors had always made him pick up the unfinished tasks of others in the department because he could not be relied on to be present all the time. The manager did not condone the absenteeism, but other than one brief conversation, decided not to make it an issue.

More than 6 years of counseling sessions had produced no improvement, so the manager decided to take 3 months to accentuate the positive and reinforce *opposite* behavior. If it didn't work, he decided he could always go back to using a "bigger two by four."

By taking this approach the manager did not take a borderline performer and help make him a superstar. But his absenteeism and lateness decreased dramatically. Other employees remarked that the individual's "attitude had improved." For the first time in a long while this employee began meeting the requirements of the job and rejoined the ranks of those considered to be "good citizens" of the company.

As the manager pointed out, if it doesn't work you can always try something else. But reinforcing opposite behavior is worth a try—especially if the behavior is not dangerous or disruptive to others. Dale Carnegie and the dozens of apostles of self-improvement techniques who have followed him testify to the power of focusing on the positive.

The world of performance can be divided into two parts. One part consists of desirable, valued behaviors you would like to see maintained or increased. The other part consists of undesirable, inappropriate behaviors you would like to see decreased or stopped. One way to decrease undesirable behavior is to reinforce opposite, incompatible, desirable behavior. The normal working day has only 8 hours. If more of those hours were spent being engaged in productive, useful, desirable behavior, there would be far less time to engage in undesirable behavior, and therefore far less undesirable behavior would occur.

Reinforcing opposite behavior can, of course, be used in conjunction with other MBC change techniques, such as prompting, modeling, and extinguishing.

Punishing Inappropriate, Undesired, Unproductive Behavior

It would be ideal if systematically using the procedures discussed so far would solve all of your "people-problems." But sometimes "accentuating the positive" just isn't enough. Some people will test an organization, a manager, or a supervisor to the limits. They will continue to engage in undesired behavior despite all the prompting and modeling of desired behavior. These people may have been reinforced for rigid, unproductive, or even disruptive patterns of behavior during most of their career. With a 15- to 20-year history of reinforcement for inappropriate behavior, it is unlikely that a few minutes of recognition and reinforcement for some unexpected (and often unplanned) achievement will turn them around. Sometimes just "catching people doing well" is not enough.

Also, certain behaviors are so serious that you do not have the time to pinpoint, track, analyze, change, and evaluate. When a towmotor operator is doing "wheelies" on the loading dock, a rational supervisor will usually go directly from pinpointing the behavior to instituting change (get off the towmotor; perhaps a fine, suspension, or termination). In such cases the change procedure of punishment may be the only effective one. But keep in mind that the term *punishment* in the MBC approach does not refer to yelling, screaming, and threatening people or calling into question an individual's heritage or genetic background. Far too often such words and procedures simply polarize the situation, making the problem worse.

MBC defines punishment as the process through which certain consequences weaken and discourage the behavior they follow. Punishers are specific consequences that decrease the likelihood of a specific behavior occurring in the future. Suppose a supervisor yells at an employee or uses criticism, embarrassment, and ridicule in an attempt to decrease some behavior. The words the supervisor uses can technically be called "punishers" only if the behavior they follow decreases. Far too often the behavior does not decrease—it may even increase. The best that can be said when the behavior does not decrease is that the supervisor tried to punish and failed. But if the behavior increases, then a more accurate description of what happened would be that the supervisor tried to punish but actually ended up reinforcing the behavior.

If you use the technique of punishment, you should work to ensure that it will be effective. Punishment, or attempts to punish, often result in serious complications and side effects. Major surgery and chemotherapy *always* produce side effects, but may or may not solve a medical problem effectively. Punishment works in the same way.

Before focusing on *when* and *how* to use punishment, let's look at the various problems, complications, and side effects associated with attempts to punish behavior.

Problems, Complications, and Side Effects Associated with Using Punishment

Punishment Produces Only a Temporary Reduction of Inappropriate Behavior

Consider the case of an employee who is spending time socializing rather than processing expense vouchers. The supervisor walks up and lectures the employee on good work attitudes. Immediately after the 3-minute scolding the employee gets back to work. However, as soon as the supervisor turns the corner, the employee starts talking about the high cost of living.

When parents say to their children, "Don't you let me catch you doing that again!" the children listen very carefully: they don't let the parents *catch* them "doing that" again. It's not that they stop "doing that." They just learn to stop for brief periods of time—when the parent is around. What a sad picture to see an organization or department functioning primarily to avoid punishment. Work gets done in spurts—spurts associated with the manager's presence. More effort is put into "watching out for the boss" than into getting the job done. Punishment is usually an inefficient method of decreasing inappropriate behavior.

Punishment Requires the Constant Presence of the Supervisor or Manager

To overcome the problem of temporary reduction of behavior, a supervisor must stand over employees almost constantly. The effectiveness of punishment depends on the presence of the punishing agent. The old saying, "When the cat's away the mice will play" is a commonsense acknowledgment of this problem. Watching over people so that punishment can be meted out if a rule is broken is a most inefficient, unproductive way for supervisory personnel to spend their time.

Punishment Does Not Teach New, More Appropriate Behavior

Think of it. How many ways are there to do a job wrong? Thousands! But there are relatively few ways to do most jobs right. If a manager's prevalent style is punitive, that manager could spend forever stomping out the thousands of potentially wrong behaviors. As soon as one inappropriate behavior is punished, another pops up to take its place.

Punishment Produces a Conditioned Emotional Response

One of the most unpleasant side effects associated with attempts to punish people is that people immediately react with what is known as the *conditioned emotional response*. This is a natural, often adaptive response for humans and animals. When a person's safety or security is threatened, when he or she is ridiculed or embarrassed or made the target of verbal abuse, that individual is conditioned to react in ways that will help him or her flee the situation or fight back if necessary. Think of a time when someone ridiculed or criticized you in front of others. Think of a time when someone cut in front of you on the highway and forced you to swerve to avoid an accident. When things like this occur, you experience a number of physical changes. Such changes include the mouth going dry, the pupils dilating, respiration increasing, perspiration increasing, acid pouring into the stomach, adrenalin secretion increasing, and blood flowing to the body's large muscles. These physiological reactions prepare you to cope with stress and danger. Is this the type of reaction you want to produce in other people? For most managers the answer is clearly "No." However, if a humanistic appeal is not convincing, consider the fact that the conditioned emotional reaction interferes with cognitive functioning—thinking and reasoning—and with eye-hand motor coordination—doing. What else do you pay people for in business but to think and do? Punishment used as a predominant method of control makes people less effective. More mistakes are made, work goes slowly, people get fatigued more easily, and organizational health suffers. It is ironic the large investment some companies make in providing their employees with "stress management" training. It would be a better investment (to say nothing of kinder!), to train the smaller number of supervisors, managers, and executives to avoid producing stressful situations in the first place.

The Emotional Side Effects of Punishment Transfer to the Presence of the Supervisor or Manager

This problem is personal to anyone who has the role of influencing others. After a while, supervisors or managers whose predominant method of controlling individuals is a punitive one are able to trigger the conditioned emotional response without saying a word. They don't have to yell, scream, or threaten. All they have to do is walk into a room, and because the sight of them has so frequently been associated with punishers, people's mouths go dry, their pupils dilate, perspiration and respiration increase, acid pours into stomachs, adrenalin is secreted, and blood flows to the large muscles. As if that's not bad enough, there is also the accompanying reduction in cognitive functioning and eye-hand motor control.

Picture a supervisor who fits this role walking by rows of workers assembling complex machinery. As the supervisor passes the first row someone's blood pressure soars; when he comes into view of the second row four people drop parts; and in the third row someone forgets to solder two wires due to his nervousness. No rational person wants to have this effect. And no company should want or allow its first-line supervisors and managers to fall into this role.

Punishment Can Produce Rigid and Inflexible Behavior Patterns

Despite the fact that punishment usually works to suppress behavior only temporarily, when it is the prevalent style of organizational influence and when the punishers are constantly present, some behavior can be inhibited permanently. For example, a supervisor may participate in a 2-day workshop on Management by Consequences and the use of recognition and reinforcement in the business setting. He then returns to work and is called to a meeting with top management to discuss ways of improving quality on the manufacturing line. At one point during the meeting the supervisor begins to suggest an idea for improvement: "Say, I just got back from a workshop where we talked about ways to influence performance. Maybe we could set up a program to provide daily feedback to employees, and the reinf . . . " and in mid-sentence an upper-level executive breaks in and says, "That's Richard for you! He goes to one workshop and thinks he can solve all our problems." This sarcastic remark embarrasses Richard, and his contribution is lost. It will take only a few instances of a punisher (the sarcastic remark) following honest suggestions for improvement to teach Richard not to make suggestions. His thoughts go something like this: "I get the picture. They don't really want suggestions. They just bring me in to feed me the party line and tell me how they're going to solve it. Okay, I'll just take care of my job; the heck with the rest of them. Let them do it the wrong way—no skin off my nose." And Richard proceeds to protect his job and his department, but never again tries to contribute to the company's overall growth, productivity, cooperation, and quality.

If the upper-level manager was confronted with the effect of his remark, he would probably protest that he hadn't meant to punish

Richard. But punishment, like reinforcement, is in the eye of the behold-
er. Certain words, such as sarcastic remarks, are more likely than others
to discourage people. If the upper-level manager had taken the time to
think about Richard's point of view, he might not have interrupted him. If
top-level managers punish creativity and risk taking, so much the worse
for the company. If a competitor's top managers are more careful with
their words and use less punishment, they just might encourage the next
million-dollar idea stifled by the other company.

In companies, organizations, and departments with high levels of
punitive measures and threats of punishment, people learn to walk the
narrow line of mediocrity. They avoid suggesting better ways of doing
things; they avoid taking risks; they avoid challenging bureaucracy and
poor decisions. Instead they fall into narrow, inflexible behavior patterns
that minimize the chance of being punished.

Punishment May Suppress or Decrease More Behavior than Planned

Consider the A-B-C sequence below.

Antecedent	Behavior	Consequence
A manufacturing engineer determines the cause of machine failure and fixes the problem in a relatively short time.	He buys a cup of coffee for the machine operator and talks happily about the successful resolution of the problem.	A manager walks by and says, "Maybe if we had a little less coffee around here, more machines would be running."

An A-B-C Sequence Showing How Punishment Can Suppress More Behavior Than Planned

In all probability that remark will serve as a punisher for the impromptu
coffee break, but the trouble with punishment is that it works like a
high-powered bullet. For example, you might be having some target
practice near your neighbor's farm. The bullet hits the bull's-eye but
continues through the target, hitting your neighbor's prize cow. His
reaction is predictable, and so is the engineer's: "I see, you solve a tough
one and they chew you out. Harry takes 2 days to troubleshoot stuff like
this and a week to fix it. I do it in 2 hours and look what I get. Harry's been
doing that for 10 years and no one ever hassles him. From now on I'll take
a week, too, and I can do that for the next 20 years."

Skillful managers understand that punishment may inhibit productive behavior and therefore use it sparingly.

Punishment May Result in Attempts at Countercontrol and
Counteraggression

When punishment is the predominant method of controlling behavior in an organization, employees learn from the model set by management. Therefore, when they seek to influence management, they too
will use fear, threats, and coercion. In addition, the conditioned emotional response they experience is often accompanied by feelings of anger
and frustration. So, even when they are not trying to influence management, this anger and frustration may be expressed in punitive ways, such
as writing graffiti, breaking and ignoring minor rules and regulations,
dressing strangely, participating in slowdowns, sabotaging work, and
even physically attacking supervisors.

You can often feel the tension between employees and management
in companies where punitive control techniques are in evidence. It can
be almost like working in an armed camp. This is the dangerous organization discussed in Chapter 7. Dangerous organizations find it difficult to
make money because so much effort goes into the disputes between
employees and managers.

In spite of these problems, side effects, and complications, many
successful managers use punishment effectively. They use it sparingly,
but when they do, they use it well. In general they are successful because
the balance they maintain between reinforcement and punishment tends
to mitigate against the emotional side effects that can result when punishment is used exclusively. When interviewed, the employees of these
managers often use the words "fair" or "tough but fair" to describe their
managers. They know their managers will provide negative consequences for poor performance, but will also provide positive consequences for good work. What skillful managers do to decrease inappropriate behavior can technically be called punishment (because it
does decrease behavior), but it is not likely to produce negative emotional
side effects because it is not viewed as a personal attack on the safety,
security, or self-esteem of the employee.

When to Use Punishment

Because attempts to decrease or stop behavior with punishment are
often accompanied by unwanted side effects and complications, some
managers and organizations find it useful to establish guidelines for
when punishment will be used. In general, following these guidelines
will help to ensure that the benefits of using punishment will outweigh
the risks.

Punishment May Be Used when the Undesired
Behavior Is Dangerous to the Person Engaging
in the Behavior

Climbing telephone poles without appropriate safety gear, wearing rings and watches while working with complex electrical equipment, entering high-voltage areas, neglecting to use protective goggles, and other unsafe behaviors often have to be stopped quickly. It would not be wise to allow such behavior to continue while waiting for prompting, reinforcing opposite behavior, or some other change procedure to have an effect. A manager has to take action immediately after such behavior occurs to ensure that it will not occur again. In such cases immediate punishment may be appropriate.

Punishment May Be Used when the Undesired Behavior Causes
Danger to Others

Operating equipment unsafely, handling food products in unhygienic ways, neglecting to monitor pressure levels in pipes carrying steam or corrosive chemicals, and assembling equipment incorrectly so that its operation may hurt the user are all examples of the kind of behavior organizations may decide to punish immediately. This seems to be a rational approach, and again, a situation where the benefits appear to outweigh the risks. Most employees understand that this type of behavior cannot be tolerated. Hard-working employees who conduct themselves safely appreciate it when management steps up to such problems. They appreciate that the company does not permit unsafe behavior and that it takes immediate action to protect them.

Punishment May Be Used when Certain Behavior Is Disruptive or
Distracting to Other Employees

Wandering around the office and engaging in lengthy, nonwork-related conversations, failing to follow procedures and thus creating more work for others, and using profane or abusive speech when dealing with others are examples of behavior that, although not dangerous, is disruptive and may be targeted for quick, punitive action. Again, this may amount to no more than a short but stern private counseling session.

Punishment May Be Used when Secrecy or Confidentiality Is Violated

Leaving confidential documents in unsecured areas, divulging company secrets, transmitting sensitive information over nonsecure telephone lines, divulging personal information, or invading an individual's privacy are examples of inappropriate actions that employees, supervisors, and managers may engage in and that some companies act swiftly to prevent from reoccurring.

Punishment May Be Used when Customers Are Treated in Ways that Might Cause Them to Stop Using the Company's Products or Services

Because customer relations are the key to any company's success, behavior that may drive customers away is dangerous to the company's welfare. Speaking rudely and abusively to customers, violating rules and procedures continuously in a customer's business location, and interfering with a customer's business or employees are behaviors that must be stopped quickly.

Punishment May Be Used when Other Change Procedures Do Not Work

Many managers and supervisors know punitive methods will work to suppress (at least temporarily) undesired behavior, but they prefer to try other procedures like prompting, reinforcing opposite behavior, and extinction first. This is especially true when the preconditions outlined in the first five guidelines for using punishment have not been met. Ultimately, though, supervisors or managers are responsible for managing the performance of their team, and this includes dealing with unsatisfactory, dangerous, or disruptive behavior. The measured approach of trying alternatives to punishment first will reduce the need for punishment; however, sometimes it must be used. Let us now look at how punishment can be used effectively in those instances where it must be used.

How to Use Punishment Effectively

Assuming that the guidelines in the previous section have been followed and we have exhausted other, more positive methods of behavior change, there are circumstances when punishing consequences must be used to decrease or stop certain behavior. Some suggestions for how to use punishment effectively are given in this section.

Decide in Advance What Consequences Will Follow the Undesired Behavior—Determine Legitimate Punishers

Most organizations realize that yelling, screaming, and using embarrassment and ridicule may work, but that their use produces too many emotional side effects and violates humane, or respectful treatment of individuals. Such consequences as fines, loss of privileges, reduction in responsibilities, assignment to a less prestigious job or location, demotion, and suspension are usually sufficient. They also help supervisors to maintain their own dignity and provide a model for nonaggressive behavior.

Punishment Should Be Made Contingent Upon Specific, Pinpointed Behaviors

You cannot punish "bad attitudes," "lack of drive," or "poor motivation." You can punish only specific behaviors. Notifying employees in advance of the specific behaviors or types of behavior that will be followed by punishing consequences is a vital step. This serves as a prompt not to engage in those behaviors and will reduce the number of times punishment actually must be used. You might consider sharing the guidelines for using punishment with employees so they know the standards their managers and supervisors use to determine the need for punishment.

Punishment Should Be Made Personal

You would not want to reinforce a team for group achievement if all members did not contribute to the achievement. It would also be grossly unfair to punish a team for the undesired behavior of one person or a few. Remember the B-O-C Audit. Personal consequences are more powerful than those that affect others.

Punishment Should Be Immediate and Should Occur as Soon After the Undesired Behavior as Possible

The longer you delay punishment, the less likely it is to have the desired effect on the behavior you are seeking to decrease. In addition, the more you delay punishment, the more likely it is that the punishing consequence will follow some bit of good performance and perhaps decrease that behavior instead.

Punishment Should Be Used Consistently

The knowledge that immediate, personal consequences are certain to follow undesired behavior often acts as a powerful deterrent. If you knew that *every time* you exceeded the speed limit on a certain highway you would be fined, you would not be likely to break the law. But because the delivery of punishment is not consistent, many people play "catch me if you can" with law enforcement authorities.

Consistency in using punishment also concerns fairness. It is unfair to give one employee a brief reprimand for a first-time safety violation while suspending another for the same first-time violation.

Punishment Should Be Followed by Reinforcement when the Desired Change in Behavior Takes Place

This final point is absolutely crucial. Why did you punish in the first place, if not to produce an improvement in performance? Once improvement takes place, you would be remiss not to use reinforcement to increase the likelihood that it will continue. If you do not use reinforcement, it is likely that another undesirable behavior will emerge to fill the void. Then you may be stuck with the need to use punishment again. Many managers report that such problems as lateness, absenteeism, and errors follow a cyclical pattern. The undesired behavior occurs, a manager uses punishment to decrease it, there is improvement for a while, but then the undesired behavior occurs again. The manager uses punishment a second time, there is temporary improvement, but then another reoccurrence. Typical of the nonreinforcing manager is: "I take action only if there's a problem; otherwise, it's not necessary. So what if he started coming in regularly and on time—he's supposed to. I pay him to be here. That's reinforcement enough. Besides, I'd have to do it for all my people."

Some managers and supervisors tackle all behavior problems this way, which is unfortunate because they will never help people to achieve their full potential in an organization. A top manager should be concerned about this because it means that the company is not getting the maximum return on its investment in human resources, and that employees are being mistreated. Management by Consequences is a way of minimizing the use of punishment. Successful, effective managers use punishment sparingly, if at all. They are often so skilled at applying the other seven change procedures that they do not have to punish. They help people achieve as much as they are capable of achieving. These managers are truly professional human resource developers.

Shaping

Shaping is a term that refers to the manager's responsibility to mold and improve performance. Just as a sculptor takes a rough piece of stone and shapes it into a beautiful work of art, a manager often must begin to work with someone who barely meets or in fact fails to meet requirements and must help that person master complex skills. Shaping is a method of teaching, and managers are teachers. *Learning* is defined as a reliable change in behavior as the result of experience. When managers help employees to learn new skills, to change their behavior, the manager is a teacher in every sense of the word.

Shaping involves taking a large, complex task, breaking it into its smaller components, and teaching each component sequentially. Later skills build on earlier skills. Shaping is the way you learn to walk, to ride a bike, ski, play tennis or golf, or fly a plane. If shaping can be used to teach the complexities of piloting an airplane, it can certainly be used to help people master business and industrial skills.

For example, a fairly high-level engineer was transferred to a new division in his company. At the new site his manager assigned him a task that required some fairly complex analytical skills. The engineer was expected to evaluate two manufacturing processes and make a recommendation on which one would be more beneficial for that particular division. After 3 weeks, the manager discovered that the engineer simply could not do the task. From his job description, salary level, and experience, he should have been able to do it, but he couldn't. So his manager had a decision to make. Should he assign this engineer to less demanding work or should he take the time to teach him (shape) the required behaviors? The manager decided that it would be better to invest the time in developing the engineer's skills. He broke the complex task into fifteen smaller steps, provided a model of how to do the first step, prompted it through verbal and written instructions, and when the first step was completed, gave positive feedback. He used the word "good," not "great" or "super" because in fact he should not have had to be this involved in the work in the first place. But he also knew that shaping required the reinforcement of small increments, of successive approximations toward the final goal.

The first assignment took three times longer than usual. But on the second assignment only five checkpoints and increments were necessary. Encouragement was given for improvement. On the third assignment the engineer soloed and did more than a satisfactory job. Shaping does take time, but the outcome is usually well worth the extra effort.

Managers are teachers, coaches, helpers, and counselors. The eight change techniques we have discussed in Chapters 9, 10 and 11, and which are summarized in Table 9, can all help in carrying out these most important roles.

You can see how the eight change procedures have been applied in a variety of settings by reading the many case histories in Appendix 1. Each history is organized around the five-step MBC approach. You will find it valuable to read each case history through the step of *analyzing*. Then before you read the *change* section, think of how you might use one or more of the eight change techniques to improve performance. Compare your approach to the one actually used in the case history.

TABLE 9 **The Eight MBC Change Techniques**

Changing Antecedents:

1. *Prompting*

    Anything you do to move another person to action is a prompt. Prompts occur before behavior and are designed to get a behavior going or to guide its direction. Rules, schedules, signs, verbal requests, orders, traffic lights, performance plans, and yellow lines on a warehouse floor are all examples of prompts. Most people have strong histories of reinforcement for responding to prompts.

2. *Modeling*

    Setting an example for someone else by your own actions is modeling. Modeling is an application of "Do as I do." Imitation is a powerful method of learning; modeling can be a powerful method of teaching.

Changing Consequences:

3. *Reinforcing*

    A reinforcer is any event that occurs after a behavior that increases the likelihood that the behavior will occur again. Three general categories of reinforcers are: *social* (people to people), *activity* (preferred tasks), and *tangible* (things, money, awards). When you systematically design work environments to make reinforcers follow appropriate behavior, you are taking advantage of this tool for change.

4. *Removing punishing consequences*

    A punisher is any event that occurs after a behavior that decreases the likelihood that the behavior will occur again. If a punisher follows desired behavior, the desired behavior may cease to occur. When you systematically design work environments to prevent punishers from following appropriate behavior, you are using this tool.

5. *Extinguishing*

    One way to decrease undesired behavior is to systematically prevent rein-

TABLE 9 **Continued**

forcers from following it. You would then be extinguishing the undesired behavior. *Note:* One explanation for the failure of desired behavior to occur is that
the desired behavior was inadvertently extinguished.

6. *Reinforcing opposite behavior*

    This is the skill of decreasing undesired behavior by "crowding it out" with
    other, opposite or incompatible behavior. For example, rather than punish
    sloppy appearance, you can reinforce neat appearance. Many managers and
    organizations find that reinforcing regular, on-time reporting to work is more
    effective than attempting to punish absenteeism or lateness.

7. *Punishing*

    Undesired behavior can be decreased or stopped by following it with
    punishing consequences. *Note:* This procedure can lead to unpleasant side
    effects, such as attempts to countercontrol, behavioral rigidity, emotional re-
    sponses, and resentment of management. It also tends to produce only tempor-
    ary suppression of the undesired behavior and does not teach new, productive
    behavior.

8. *Shaping*

    Shaping breaks a complex task into smaller steps; it combines several
    previous steps (prompting, modeling, reinforcing, removing punishing con-
    sequences, and extinguishing) to teach new behavior. Shaping is the way
    people learn to ride a bike, to ski, or to fly an airplane. It is a powerful tool for
    change. Shaping also involves the ability to reinforce successive approxima-
    tions to a goal, even though the goal has not yet been reached. Once the
    desired goal is attained, the external support can be faded out and the natural
    reinforcers for doing a complex job well can take over.

SELF-TEACHING EXERCISE

After reading each of the case histories that follow, indicate how
some aspect(s) of the MBC approach could be applied to help solve the
problem outlined. Although you will not have enough information to
conduct a complete A-B-C Analysis or B-O-C Audit, suggest some possible things to look for. How can the five-step MBC approach be applied?
Which of the eight change procedures might be tried? What principles
covered in Chapters 9, 10, and 11 are involved (e.g., side effects of
punishment, rules for using reinforcers, etc.)?

Case 1: A manager in a large chemical processing plant tells a first-
line supervisor that his poor attitude and negativism are unsatisfactory.
The manager says that unless there is a definite improvement, the supervisor may be terminated. One month later the supervisor is fired and he
complains that he doesn't understand why.

How does the MBC approach apply? What suggestions would you
make for improvement?

Case 2: The president of a bank with eight branch offices notices that there is a wide disparity in performance and morale between two of the offices in particular. At Branch A, turnover is at a minimum, the ratio of accounts opened to accounts closed is at or above the company average, and the manager seems happy. At Branch B, there is a high rate of staff turnover, a declining number of accounts, and some dissension among the employees and between the employees and the manager. The manager acknowledges that the staff's overall performance and morale are not what they could be, and feels that the best approach is to keep one step ahead of them by coming down hard in general and "reaming them out" at monthly staff meetings. "You've got to keep them guessing to keep them working," was one of the remarks he made to the company president.

How does the MBC approach apply? What suggestions would you make for improvement?

Case 3: In a large city hospital thousands of dollars worth of supplies go unaccounted for each month because nurses, nurses' aides, and volunteers fail to properly record the names of the patients to whom consumable items are delivered. The head nurses and unit chiefs report that they criticize the staff frequently for these omissions, and one unit chief even uses the intercom system to announce each month's losses, along with a stern warning about the dire effects these continual losses can have on fiscal solvency. The hospital administrator reports that theft is not a problem, but that his accounting system is being thrown into disarray because he is unable to keep track of these consumable items.

How does the MBC approach apply? What suggestions would you make for improvement?

Case 4: Tom Hale, a marketing representative for a large computer firm, is being considered for the position of branch office manager at another location. His present boss, as well as one of the division vice-presidents, feels that he has the requisite skills but that there is one thing standing in his way. At department meetings Tom frequently interrupts others with one-liners, wisecracks, and sarcastic remarks. His boss reports that he is an extremely bright, articulate, and witty individual, but that these remarks are disrupting the meetings and affecting Tom's credibility. The division president feels he is too immature to manage a branch office. Tom's manager has spoken to him several times about this problem on an informal basis and asked him to stop the disruptive behavior, but instead the interruptions appear to be occurring as often as ever. In addition, Tom has told his manager that he picked the habit up in college, that it's hard to change, and besides, he thinks his remarks are pretty funny.

How does the MBC approach apply? What suggestions would you make for improvement?

Case 5: A forklift operator in a trucking firm is beginning to develop unsafe driving habits. Over the past 3 years this individual has received several promotions and has worked his way up from an entry-level position to his present high pay and high status job. However, his dock supervisor reports that he is now beginning to drive in an unsafe manner, such as backing up without sounding his horn, speeding, taking corners too closely, and picking up too many pallets at one time, often to the applause of other employees on the loading dock. His supervisor is disappointed at this deterioration in performance because the operator rose rapidly to the highest status position on the loading dock and in the past his driving was always exemplary. Informal warnings and several stern counseling sessions have not produced any improvement, and in fact there have been an increasing number of dangerous driving incidents over the past few weeks.

How does the MBC approach apply? What suggestions would you make for improvement?

Some Possible Answers

Case 1: It appears that the manager may not have pinpointed. Words like "poor attitude" and "negativism" are not sufficient grounds for firing someone in most companies.

Both the manager and supervisor should be interviewed to see if pinpointing took place. If it did not, the supervisor deserves to know the behaviors that are unsatisfactory. Telling the supervisor in specific terms what behavior is inappropriate is a form of prompting. If improvement takes place, reinforcement should be used. The manager should be encouraged to pinpoint with all supervisors. The MBC decision-making process could also be helpful here.

Case 2: Pinpointing is needed. There may be a negative reaction to punishment in Branch B.

Direct observations of both branch managers would help to identify pinpointed behaviors of the managers and employees. If any differences are found, branch manager B could be encouraged to try some of the words and procedures being used by manager A.

Case 3: Punishment seems to be the major method of influence here. There may also be a need for pinpointing and specific performance standards.

Head nurses and unit chiefs should be encouraged to reinforce appropriate behavior. Tracking and providing feedback in the form of publicly posted numbers or a chart showing total dollars unaccounted for could influence employees. Any punishments for proper recording should be removed.

Case 4: The use of the word "immature" and the informal talks on "disruptive behavior" may indicate lack of pinpointing. Tom may be getting reinforcement from the laughter of his peers and the informal discussion.

Tom's boss should pinpoint the inappropriate behaviors. Tom and his boss could privately track how many times the behavior actually occurs in a meeting. The tracking itself might serve to decrease it. Tom's boss should be careful not to laugh at the one-liners and other remarks. He may be *modeling* laughter for Tom's peers. Tom can be told the consequences that will occur if he continues to disrupt meetings. These consequences may currently be in the other, delayed, and uncertain categories as far as Tom's awareness is concerned. Telling Tom will make the consequences of his behavior more personal, immediate, and certain to him. Tom's boss might try keeping a serious expression on his face after Tom interrupts. This will model nonlaughing for Tom's peers, and if they stop laughing the remarks should *extinguish.* Tom can be reinforced for pertinent remarks he makes and other forms of appropriate behavior.

Case 5: The criteria for using punishment seem to be fulfilled here. This is a dangerous behavior that must be stopped. The operator may be getting reinforcement from his peers for dangerous actions. Since his last promotion to the highest status position, management may no longer be reinforcing him for safe driving.

Swift action should be taken. Tom may be removed from the towmotor or suspended for some period. This may work as a punishment for the unsafe driving. After a period, Tom can be reassigned to the towmotor to see if there is improvement. If improvement does occur, the supervisor should reinforce him for good performance.

CHAPTER TWELVE
EVALUATING YOUR EFFECTIVENESS

The value of any approach to management can be judged by the answer to the question "What difference does it make?" If a particular change procedure is effective, then the frequency of a pinpointed behavior should be different following institution of the change procedure from the baseline frequency established during the tracking phase. It is important to continue tracking the pinpointed behavior after the change phase of any project so that you can compare the prechange period with the postchange period. This before and after comparison will show you how much influence you are having and how much progress has been made by the person you are attempting to influence.

If the project is successful, the changing numbers will also reinforce you for trying the MBC approach. You shouldn't be discouraged, however, if there is no change; this simply means that the current antecedents and consequences are not powerful enough or that other change techniques (you have eight to choose from) should be tried.

You will find a performance improvement work action plan outlined on page 136. Space is provided for you to indicate the pinpointed behavior of concern as well as the method of tracking. You can also indicate what change procedure(s) your analysis leads you to. By completing the section titled "Evaluate," you will set a goal for behavior change and demonstrate the economic payoff to your company and the individual involved. Examples of economic payoffs, such as reduced scrap, rework, and absenteeism, and increased sales, production, and quality, are included in Appendix 1.

Not every project results in an improvement that can be measured in dollars. When managers and supervisors use reinforcement to influence behavior, the side effects and complications associated with punishment are avoided. This can result in an increase in employee satisfaction, as measured by an attitude survey. Many companies feel this improvement in satisfaction or "morale" translates into economic benefits, such as

Performance Improvement Work Action Plan

```
 _____         _____
          Name                           Position
1. Pinpoint
   Behavior _____

   _____
   Where exhibited _____
   How performance related _____
   (output measure?)
2. Track
   How counted _____
   Where counted _____
   When and for how long _____
3. Analyze (see A-B-C Analysis and/or B-O-C Audit)
4. Change
   Indicate your proposed intervention strategy. (This will include changes
   in either antecedents, consequences, or both.)

   _____
   _____
   _____
   _____
   Starting date _____
   Duration _____
5. Evaluate
   Description of amount of change which will be deemed satisfactory
   (standards or goals)

   _____
   Cost-effectiveness measures (economic payoffs) _____
```

decreased turnover, absenteeism, and time lost resolving interpersonal problems.

Fewer vague, often derogatory labels and a decreased use of punishment can create a less stressful environment. This in turn can result in less stress-related illness and absenteeism.

What If the Behavior Does Not Change?

There will be times when all your attempts to help someone improve will not result in change in the desired direction. Your only choice then will be to decide how important it is to you, to the company, and to the employee to change the behavior. If it is important, then probably only a radical change in the environment will work. The most radical change, of course, is firing an employee. This may help the company and you. It may also be a favor to the employee, but even if it isn't, your choices are not unlimited. Managers who follow the five steps of MBC, employ the decision-making process, and try the eight change techniques, can usually justify firing someone. They have done all they can to help that individual, but the employee has chosen not to live up to the employment agreement. To keep an employee under such circumstances would simply reinforce undesired behavior.

Another option you have is to reevaluate whether it really is worth trying to change the individual's behavior. The costs versus the benefits of the change may indicate that if a simple attempt to influence the person does not work, more involved techniques would not be worth it. You simply decide to live with some things because the individual's contributions are too important to jeopardize. This option is also used when the person whose behavior we are trying to change is a peer or a superior. In that case, however, we are saying that the costs to us or the risks to us are too great, so we will live with it.

If the first two options are unacceptable to you, a third option would be to transfer an employee to another job. In many companies there are enough jobs so that this is practical. However, it is important that the transfer not be characterized as a reward or greater opportunity. This would be likely to reinforce whatever undesirable behavior was occurring. In some cases supervisors give poor performers high appraisals so that they can transfer them. This helps the supervisor, but it does not usually help the employee or the company. This option is not useful if the person you are trying to influence is a peer or someone at a higher level in your organization.

The only other option you have if your attempt to influence someone is not successful is to quit your job or get a transfer yourself. If a pinpointed behavior is so inappropriate, so distasteful, so disturbing to you that you cannot live with it or pursue other options, then all you can do is remove yourself from the situation. (Contemplating this option often focuses us back on previous options.)

What If Someone Else in Your Organization Reads this Book?

If you find other people—perhaps someone you report to—being more specific, avoiding labels, and asking you exactly what you mean when you use words like "attitude," "drive," and "motivation," they may have read this book. If you notice them referring more often to directly observable behavior and measurable end results, this could also be an indication that they have read this book. If someone you know begins to analyze problems using phrases like "Well, we may have been reinforcing their inappropriate behavior," or "Have you considered the punishing consequences that occur when their reports are turned in on time?", your suspicion that this person has read this book might be justified. If someone starts giving you the credit and recognition you've always felt you deserved, it might very well be that he or she has read this book. But that's all right—we are always influencing one another. The only question is what *techniques* we will use.

If you think someone is trying to influence you using principles discussed in this book, ask them what pinpointed behavior of yours they would like to see changed. Find out what reinforcers they have available or what punishers they can remove to help you improve. Perhaps they can reinforce you by changing a pinpointed behavior of their own—that is what win/win negotiations are all about. MBC is based on sound principles of human behavior and is consistent with showing respect for all individuals.

A Final Word

In the final analysis, what does the MBC approach have to say about managing behavior on the job? *Pinpointing* says simply that successful leaders are specific and explicit in communicating job expectations to others. They do not label. They involve their subordinates in determining what pinpointed behaviors will be used to achieve objectives and end results.

Tracking emphasizes that effective supervisors not only know and communicate *what* is expected, but *how much*. They understand the need for standards of performance and communicate these standards clearly. As with pinpointing, they are comfortable with involving employees in determining these standards. They realize that the majority of workers appreciate an opportunity to help determine what they do and how they will do it.

Analyzing ensures that a manager will not charge off to fix something that is not broken. The best managers work efficiently. They determine the cause(s) of a problem before making changes. They avoid making inferences and assumptions about the causes of behavior. Good managers are not locked into one rigid view of why people behave as they do. They are willing to consider a number of possibilities. They understand that a wide variety of environmental factors can affect performance and attempt to determine the impact of each systematically.

Changing the environment in some way to encourage changes in behavior is something successful managers have always done. Effective leaders have a large repertoire of procedures for influencing others and are not tied to a single method that used once without success leaves them helpless.

Evaluating the effectiveness of any procedure is crucial to success. Good managers know when they have succeeded, and deserve the credit. They also know when they have not been successful, but because they are not locked into a single solution, they can try again with another of a variety of change techniques.

Managing behavior on the job is what supervisors, managers, and executives are paid to do. I have personally found this role to be one of the most interesting and rewarding experiences of my life. I have found, along with hundreds of other managers, that the principles and procedures of Management by Consequences work, and work well. I hope you find that they work for you. I wish you success.

APPENDIX ONE
PRACTICAL APPLICATIONS OF THE MBC APPROACH

Case 1: Decreasing Number of Errors on Accounts Payable Vouchers

Pinpoint. Making errors on accounts payable vouchers.

Track. The supervisor of two groups of employees in the accounts payable department of a large restaurant chain tracked the number of errors made by each group for 1 week. Group 1 made twenty-five errors, group 2 made fifteen.

Analyze. The antecedent for the errors was simply preparing accounts payable vouchers. On the other hand, the consequence was difficult to identify because the employees did not know when they made errors. The mistakes were typically corrected by someone else.

Change. For the first 2 weeks the supervisor merely mentioned that he would be measuring the number of errors and providing each group with feedback on their performance. After 2 weeks, a standard of four errors per week was set as the goal. If the group of workers made four errors or fewer, the supervisor would take them to lunch.

Evaluate. Results for each group are shown on page 142. Employees quickly reduced their errors and achieved the performance standard. After receiving the consequence of being taken to lunch, a new procedure was instituted. If the department achieved a goal of one error or less per week per employee for a period of 4 weeks, then each employee would receive some time off. Meeting the goal for 8 weeks would result in additional time off plus free food coupons. After 1 year of operation, the program continued to be successful. One employee was able to maintain a standard of one error or less per week for 30 weeks. Each group main-

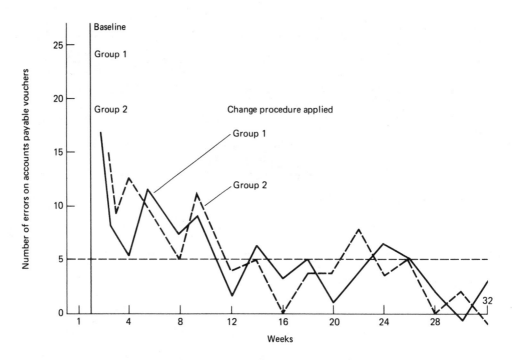

Decreasing Number of Errors on Accounts Payable Vouchers

tained the standard of four or fewer errors for most weeks. Savings of between $150 and $200 per month were realized by the company as it no longer had to correct as many errors.

A related measure of number of customer service calls dealing with incorrect payment of bills showed that such calls dropped from sixty-three to fifteen per month. The company estimated direct and indirect savings as a result of the simple change in consequences at approximately $1000 per month. The restaurant chain used similar incentive plans to reduce the errors in managers' cash reports received from some 150 different retail units. The company was able to reduce its audit fee by $10,000 from the estimated amount and negotiate a 16 percent reduction in the audit fee for the following year.

Reference. Rettig, E. B. How to reduce costly "mis-takes" in a steak house, Work Performance 2(3):4–8, January 1975.

Case 2: Reduction of Cash Shortages in a Family-Style Restaurant

Pinpoint. Making errors in giving customers their change and/or theft.

Track. Six of the fifteen employees at the restaurant worked as cashiers. On any given day, a minimum of three and a maximum of six cashiers used either of two cash registers to ring up sales. The total amount of cash in both registers was compared to the combined total of the two register tapes each day to determine whether a discrepancy existed. This method of tracking did not require the hiring of private detectives, extra security personnel, or use of surveillance cameras or "lie detectors." Baseline data were collected for 5 days.

Analyze. The antecedent was identified simply as working at the cash register. There were no systematic consequences for making errors, except possibly the money itself, if a cash shortage was the result of theft.

Change. Following establishment of the baseline, cashiers were told that if any single day's cash shortages equaled or exceeded 1 percent of that day's sales receipts, the total shortage divided by the number of cashiers working that day would be subtracted from each cashier's salary for that particular day. This is a "response-cost" procedure which entails removal of a reinforcer following an undesired behavior. After 18 days the procedure was discontinued, and then reinstituted on day 21 for an additional 21 days.

Evaluate. The illustration on page 144 shows the average cash shortages during each phase of the project. The baseline period average daily shortage was 4.02 percent of the day's receipts. Implementing the response-cost procedure resulted in an immediate drop to an average daily shortage of 0.43 percent. During the first 12 days, employees were fined only on the 2 days when shortages exceeded the criterion of 1 percent. When the response-cost procedure was removed, the percentage of cash shortages immediately increased to an average of over 4 percent. When the procedure was reinstated, there was a reduction in cash shortages to 0.04 percent during the 21 days of the final phase. No workers were fined as shortages never exceeded the 1 percent criterion.

It is important to note that employees had the opportunity to express their displeasure with the procedure, but did not. Ethical considerations should govern whether such a procedure is appropriate in other settings. A reinforcement program might have worked as well. At any rate, the procedures involved may still have been more desirable than the alternatives of group surveillance and lie detectors, which would typically result in harsher treatment of offenders. The change in antecedents, involving the open, clear statement of new rules coupled with fines for only 3 days at a total cost of only $8.70 per cashier, resulted in a significant reduction of cash shortage.

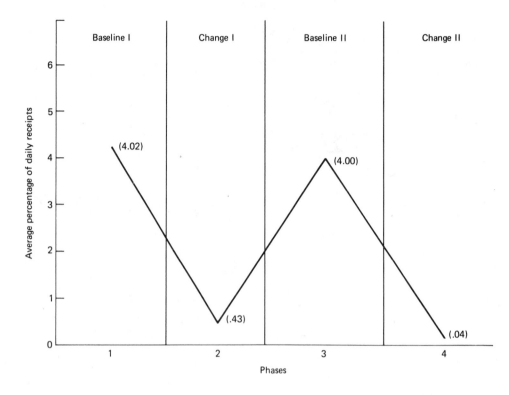

Average Cash Shortages

Reference. Marholin, D. and Gray, D. Effects of group response-cost procedure on cash shortages in a small business, *Journal of Applied Behavior Analysis* 9:25–30, 1976.

Case 3: Reduction of "Peaking" in Residential Electrical Energy Consumers in Seattle, Washington

---

Pinpoint. Using electrical appliances and devices at high rates for brief periods during the day.

Track. Peaking results in the inefficient use of generating facilities and may force the use of older, less safe, and more environmentally damaging facilities in the Seattle area. Residential consumption is 40 percent of the total electrical energy produced. The morning peak begins at 8:00 a.m. and runs to 1:00 p.m. The afternoon peak is between 6:00 and 8:00 p.m.

A current-sensitive relay was installed in each of three homes, which turned on a signal light when current levels exceeded the criterion level that would indicate "peaking." This device served both to track and provide feedback on the electrical energy-consuming behavior of the three families involved in the project.

Change. For one phase of the procedure the signal light that provided immediate feedback on excess energy use was used alone. In another phase monetary incentives were tied to the reduction of peaking.

Evaluate. The feedback condition using the signal light alone resulted in approximately a 20 percent reduction in peaking, whereas a combination of feedback plus incentives was most effective and reduced peaking by about 50 percent. Reports from the families involved revealed that the procedure provided them with information on how their daily behavior habits related to peaking. For example, the immediate feedback of the signal light showed that one could reduce peaking by not turning on the dishwasher until just before bedtime. All three families reported the most difficulty in controlling behaviors that resulted in the use of hot water. Nevertheless, the project did show that immediate availability of information on electrical energy consumption was important in producing behavior change.

Reference. Kohlenberg, R., Phillips, T., and Proctor, W. A behavioral analysis of peaking in residential electrical-energy consumers. *Journal of Applied Behavior Analysis* 9:13–18, 1976.

Case 4: Increasing New Warranty Sales in a Large Canadian Industrial Firm

Pinpoint. Making warranty sales over the phone for household and garden appliances.

Track. Two individuals were hired to sell service contracts on household and garden appliances for a large industrial firm. However, the salesmen preferred to make renewal calls rather than calls to sell new service contracts. Tracking of calls in each category was accomplished by providing the salesmen with stacks of cards containing both renewal and new service contract leads, and then noting which calls were made. Baseline data were collected for 10 days, and showed that the salesmen were calling many more renewal customers than new prospects.

Analyze. The stacks of cards served as the antecedent to the pinpointed behavior. Because renewal contracts are easier to sell than new contracts, it is likely that the greater success achieved in selling renewal contracts functioned as a strong positive consequence for making calls to renewal customers.

Change. As the preferred activity of the salesmen was calling renewal prospects, it was decided to make the opportunity to make five such calls dependent on selling one new warranty contract. Thus, in order to make five calls to renewal prospects, the salesmen had to sell one new contract first. This procedure of requiring someone to exhibit a less-preferred behavior before permitting him to exhibit a more-preferred behavior is called *activity reinforcement.*

Evaluate. The illustration on page 147 shows the percentages of new and renewal sales. The total sales of each type *each day* were divided by the total calls of each type daily. During the baseline phase, renewal sales were at about 30 percent and exceeded new sales by a ratio of approximately 3:1.

When the change procedure was introduced, the percentage of sales for *each* type of contract increased. When the procedure was stopped after 10 days, there was a slight drop in renewal sales for one salesman (1 percent) and a drastic drop for the other (21 percent). New contract sales dropped to zero. When the reinforcement ceased, the behavior of making less-preferred sales calls ceased.

Reference. Gupton, T. and LeBow, M. D. Behavior management in a large industrial firm, *Behavior Therapy* 2:78–83, 1971.

Case 5: Reducing Absenteeism in a Large Manufacturing and Distribution Center

---

Pinpoint. Coming to work.

Track. Attendance at work was recorded for each employee.

Analyze. No single antecedent or consequence was identified as influencing absenteeism consistently.

Change. A lottery incentive system was developed in which an employee was allowed to choose one card from a deck of playing cards on the days he or she came to work on time. At the end of a 5-day week, the employee from each department (average size: 25 workers) with the winning poker hand would win $20.

Evaluate. Absenteeism dropped from an average of 3.01 to 2.46 percent, a decrease of 18.27 percent. When the procedure was stopped, absenteeism climbed back to 3.02 percent after 22 weeks. Upon reinstituting the procedure, absenteeism immediately dropped to 2.4 percent and stayed at that level for 6 weeks.

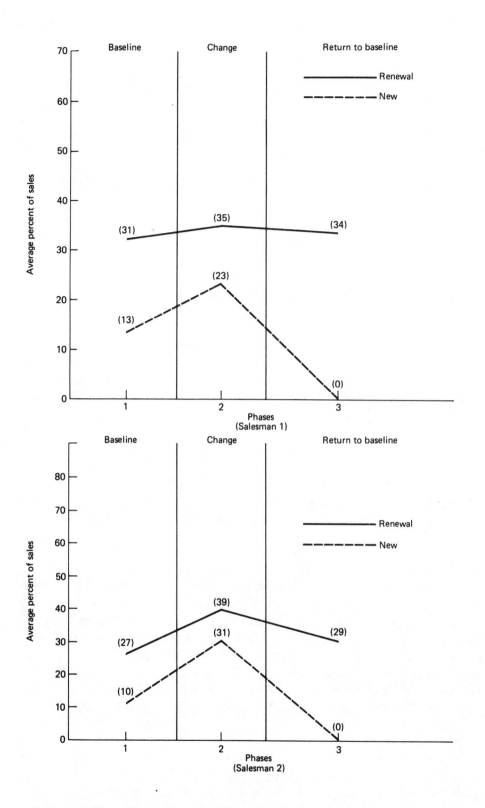

Percentages of New and Renewal Sales

Reference. Pedalino, E., and Gamboa, V. Behavior modification and absenteeism: Intervention in one industrial setting. *Journal of Applied Psychology* 59:694–698, 1974.

Case 6: Increasing Punctuality of Industrial Workers in Mexico City

---

Pinpoint. Reporting to work and clocking in on time.

Track. Records were kept of attendance at work and punctuality for each employee.

Analyze. This industrial plant employing 131 workers in Mexico City experienced 750 separate instances of lateness in 1 year. The company had used a system of bonuses and sanctions in an attempt to improve this situation. The bonus system included a bonus of 500 pesos ($40) for the ten workers who had the best punctuality and attendance records over a year. Ten yearly awards of 400 pesos ($32) and twenty in the amount of 300 pesos ($24) were given to the next lowest workers. Unfortunately, this long delay between the appropriate behavior (coming to work on time) and the consequence (yearly bonus) was not as effective as the company would have liked. In addition, sanctions were imposed on workers who were chronically late. A worker might be suspended for a day or sent home if late. Again, there was often a long delay between lateness and suspension.

Change. It was decided to employ an immediate reinforcement procedure for each day a worker reported on time. The workers chosen for the pilot project had a record of chronic lateness for the previous year. The procedure involved telling each worker that he would receive a slip of paper worth two pesos (16¢) for each day he clocked in on time or early. At the end of each week he could exchange the slips for cash. If a worker was late, he would not receive a punctuality bonus for that day. The union had been informed of the project and union officials raised no objections.

Evaluate. The results for various phases of the project, during which the procedure was put into effect, then stopped, reinstated, stopped, and then reinstated again are shown on the opposite page. The workers were also compared with another group of workers who did not experience the new procedure. This control group demonstrated a much higher incidence of lateness.

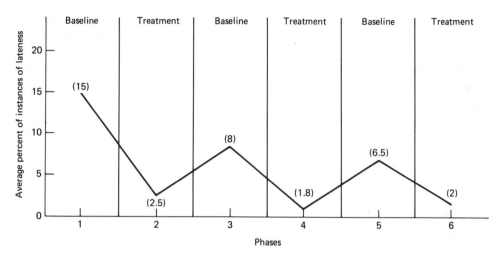

Instances of Lateness

Reference. Hermann, J. A., de Montes, A. I., Dominguez, B., Montes, F., and Hopkins, B. L. Effects of bonuses for punctuality on the tardiness of industrial workers, *Journal of Applied Behavior Analysis* 6:563–570, 1973.

Case 7: Increasing the Number of Job Openings Reported by Community Residents to the Illinois State Employment Service, and the Number of Job Placements Made by the Employment Service

---

Pinpoint. Notifying the placement service of a state employment office of job openings.

Track. The placement service kept track of the number of job openings reported by community residents as well as the number of subsequent job placements.

Analyze. An analysis of how unemployed workers find jobs indicated that fully two-thirds of the job leads come from friends or relatives who (1) know of specific job openings, (2) were employed by the hiring firm, and/or (3) actively influenced the hiring by speaking to individuals in the hiring firm. An attempt was made to motivate community residents to report unpublicized openings, which a survey showed was the largest source of jobs.

Change. An advertisement was placed in the local paper offering a reward for information on job openings that led to the employment of one of the employment service's job applicants. This was compared with the results obtained from a similar ad that solicited information on job openings but did not offer a reward. The reward procedure paid $100 to the provider of the information. A payment of $25 was made to the caller at the time an applicant was hired. Three additional payments of $25 would then be made at the end of each of the applicant's first 3 weeks of successful employment.

Evaluate. The reward procedure resulted in ten times as many job leads and eight times as many placements as the no-reward advertisement. The average cost per placement was $130 using the reward procedure, as compared with $470 per placement with the no-reward procedure. There was no evidence that the jobs were marginal, temporary, or undesirable. All were full-time jobs at above the legal minimum wage (about $500 per month in 1972–1973). There was no evidence of attempts to circumvent the procedure by firing the employees after the reward period.

Reference. Jones, R. J., and Azrin, N. H. An experimental application of a social reinforcement approach to the problem of job-finding. *Journal of Applied Behavior Analysis* 6:345–353, 1973.

Case 8: Increasing the Number of Daily Customer Service Behaviors and Routine Tasks in Five Family Steak Houses

---

Pinpoint. Standard customer service behavior included taking orders, laying out trays, collecting tickets, cooking, delivering the meal, asking the customers if they were pleased during the meal, and saying "thank you" before customers left. Standard routine tasks in the kitchen and dining room were taken from the company's operations manual and included cooking, cleaning, preparing meats, washing dishes, and bussing trays.

Track. Customer service was measured by designating an employee to measure eleven customer service behaviors which were listed on a 3 × 5 inch size card (see Pinpoint). A time sampling method was used. Sample observations were made ten times daily. A percentage of customer service behaviors performed by a group of workers was posted on a bulletin board each day.

Analyze. No clear performance goals had ever been specified prior to the project, nor had specific behaviors been pinpointed for the employees so that they knew exactly what was expected of them.

Change. After baseline data had been collected, the employees and manager in each of the five restaurants agreed on a performance goal for the following week. On days when the employees met or exceeded performance standards, all employees could draw from a deck of cards. After 5 days on which performance standards were met, the employee with the winning poker hand won a small bonus.

Evaluate. The top portion of the illustration on page 152 shows the results for one restaurant in which customer service performance rose from 68 to 90 percent of standard after 2 months. A similar program of checklists of pinpointed behaviors was used for routine tasks in various areas of each restaurant (see Pinpoint). The bottom part shows these results in another restaurant. One positive side effect of these procedures was the increased involvement of employees in supervising their own performance. Restaurant managers took an active role as teachers of appropriate behavior and true human resource managers. Prior to the initiating of the behavioral approaches outlined, many employees complained about the workload. Following the intervention program, many asked for more responsibilities.

Reference. Rettig, E. B. How to reduce costly "mis-takes" in a steak house, *Work Performance* 2(3):4–8, January 1975.

Case 9: Increasing Productivity of Central Delivery Service and Office Credit Department of a Chain of Australian Retail Stores

Pinpoint. Attempting deliveries; returning undelivered merchandise to warehouse; damaging freight; reporting for work; and processing documents in a clerical department.

Track. Careful records were kept of each of the behaviors listed under Pinpoint.

Analyze. Prior to the start of the project, there was a serious deterioration in the pinpointed behaviors listed. This was caused partly by rapid expansion of the company and centralization of warehousing and shipping. With centralization, the drivers' performance went largely unrecorded and unrecognized. The company was plagued with work stoppages, damaged freight, a low number of deliveries, and many complaints from drivers.

Change. After pinpointing and tracking the behaviors listed, detailed feedback and recognition of performance improvement was provided to each individual driver. Any improvement was followed by a note of congratulations and appreciation from the warehouse manage-

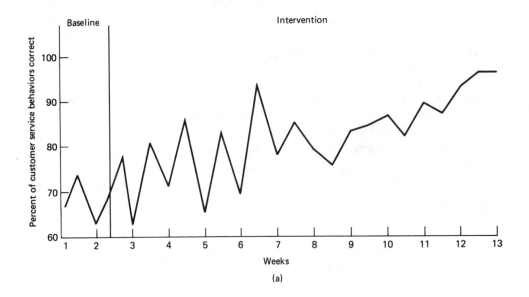

(a)

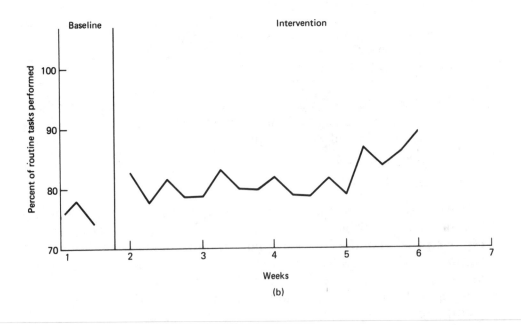

(b)

Performance Results for Customer Service Behaviors and Routine Tasks

ment, along with verbal praise whenever possible. No other incentives or rewards were used.

Evaluate. There was significant improvement in all areas, and after 20 months of operation this improvement had been maintained. Attendance at work increased as did the number of deliveries attempted, and percentage of damaged freight was down. The company recorded an overall 30 percent increase in productivity in this area. In addition, work stoppages were eliminated and the ratio of wages to output was reduced from 5.6 to 3.9 percent in 1 year. The company extended the program to the entire warehouse with similar results.

When applied to its head office Credit Department, the measure used was total number of documents held divided by the average weekly number of invoices processed. By using pinpointing, tracking, and feedback with social reinforcement, the ratio of unprocessed documents to processed ones fell from 112 to 0.28 per week.

Reference. Mitchell, B. The Australian story. *Performance Improvement* 1(6):1–4, April 1976.

Case 10: Reducing the Scrap Rate of a Machine Shop Team in a Manufacturing Plant

---

Pinpoint. Stopping the stamping mill when a defective piece is identified, and sharpening and realigning the dies.

Track. The team supervisor took a baseline measure of the group's scrap rate for a 2-week period.

Analyze. The supervisor had attempted to reduce the group scrap rate once before by posting equipment maintenance rules and reminding workers about procedures. This had had little effect. After pinpointing the behaviors he wanted to increase and tracking them for 2 weeks, he now decided to introduce a new consequence.

Change. The new consequence for the workers' performance was simply a chart showing the scrap rate, which was posted in the department work area. The supervisor also solicited suggestions from the workers on how to improve scrap rate.

Evaluate. The consequences of providing feedback and implementing suggestions worked to improve productivity, as shown in the

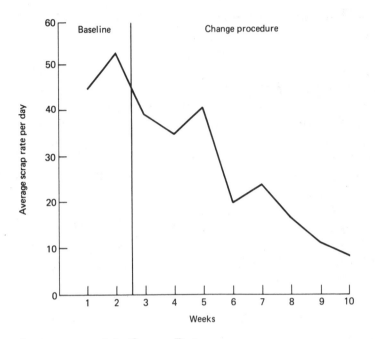

Improvement in Scrap Rate

illustration above. A pleasant side effect of this procedure was an increased level of interaction between the supervisor and his workers.

Reference. Luthans, F. and Kreitner, R. *Organizational Behavior Modification*, Scott Foresman, Glenview, Ill. pp. 154–155, 1975.

Case 11: Increasing the Number of Requisitions Filled in an Automated Warehouse

Pinpoint. Increasing the number of requisitions filled.

Track. To establish a baseline, the manager tracked the number of requisitions filled by each employee. He tracked on a daily basis for several days.

Analyze. The manager's baseline data showed a department average of ten requisitions filled per hour. However, some employees were filling as many as fifteen, while others were only filling five, despite the fact that all employees handled the same material.

Change. With the baseline information in hand, the manager called the department members together and they mutually established a goal of fifteen requisitions per hour. All involved felt such a goal was reasonable. The only request made by the employees was that a contingency be built into the system that would take into account mechanical failures. The manager assured everyone that this had been done. He also informed them that he was using a 7.2-hour day rather than an 8-hour day in calculating daily goals. A new system of posting the total number of requisitions filled by the entire team was also established to provide feedback. This feedback was a new consequence for filling requisitions.

Evaluate. The graph below outlines the results of the project. Prior to the meeting, the department as a group had been averaging 420 requisitions per day. On the day following the meeting, 520 requisitions were recorded; within a week the number had risen to over 600, and by the middle of the second week 648 requisitions per day were attained. At that time the manager asked his upper-level manager to address the department members, to compliment them on their effort and improvement and to single out the highest performer for special attention. This recognition from upper management was another new consequence for good performance.

In the manager's opinion, several benefits resulted from the department meeting he held: (1) specific productivity goals were jointly established; (2) friendly competition was stimulated among department mem-

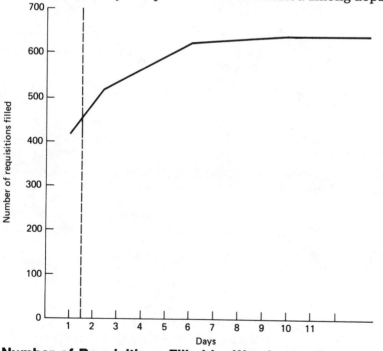

Number of Requisitions Filled by Warehouse Employees

bers and the rate of requisition filling continued to increase, finally peaking at twenty per hour; and (3) the employees felt that management was finally recognizing the good performers.

One concern that was expressed as the requisition-filling rate continued to grow had to do with the quality of work. However, it was found that quality, as measured by number of errors in filling requisitions, improved slightly. The manager reported this as a "pleasant surprise." The manager's report of his project indicated that:

> "Department morale seems to be very high. There is continuous praise for the department and the employees. The employees take real pride in their accomplishments. Many have been promoted. All accomplishments were without the aid of tools or additional cost to the company. Everything was there that was needed. It was simply a matter of capitalizing on the best resources—people."

Source. Personal communication, line manager.

Case 12: Decreasing Errors and Rework Rate on Design Drawings and Other Documents in the Development Laboratory of a High Technology Company

---

Pinpoint. Decreasing errors and rework rate on design drawings.

Track. The manager's department consisted of two shifts of draftsmen and designers. He tracked the average rework rate for his department as a whole and found it to be 55 percent.

Analyze. At this point the manager was convinced that the designers were making so many errors because they were "lazy, unmotivated, (had) a bad attitude and simply (didn't) care." However, after being encouraged to analyze the effect that current antecedents and consequences were having on his employees' performance, he realized some interesting things about his own management practices:

- *After* an individual employee was identified as making many mistakes, the manager held a one-on-one counseling session to bring the problem to the employee's attention.
- *After* department-wide errors increased to a certain level (as measured by complaints from user groups), he held a department meeting to discuss errors, mistakes, sloppiness, and rework.

The manager reported that the one-on-one sessions produced some temporary improvement, but that the problem was cyclical. After a few weeks or months the rate would again begin to rise and he would once more have to hold individual and group meetings.

The manager realized that he was providing many consequences for poor performance, but no systematic consequences for good performance. Yet there was good performance! When using a group measure, at least 45 percent of the time some employees made almost no errors. He had reported earlier that he knew he had some good people: "Thank heavens for them, but it's the problem employees I find myself spending all my time with."

The manager saw that:

• His current management practices were not working very well.
• His assumption that several of his people were lazy and unmotivated was just that—an assumption.
• His current set of consequences was at best weak and at worst working in the wrong direction.
• He was not systematically providing consequences for good performance.

Change. Based on this analysis, the manager made some very specific changes in his management practices and style, the first of which was predicted to reduce the company to bankruptcy within 30 days! This change was to have the employees correct their own errors. The manager agreed that there probably was not enough time to correct their own errors under the current system. However, the present system also had a 55 percent rework problem because the first available employee had been making the corrections; thus, first-shift employees frequently corrected second-shift errors, and vice versa. Such a procedure often resulted in animosity between individuals and shifts, with each shift feeling that its personnel was carrying the company while the other shift was dragging it down.

The manager was determined to try the new procedure because his analysis of the current situation impressed him with the need for better feedback systems. If employees did not know of their mistakes, how could they be expected to improve? Seeing their own errors might help. In addition, because most errors appeared to result from carelessness, employees might take a little more time if they knew they were sure to get the job back if mistakes were found. In his analysis of the system, the manager had found that many employees were aware of the *number* of documents they processed, but not their quality.

He also made some very specific changes in his own management style. His analysis showed much attention being paid to errors, but little attention and few positive consequences for good performance. The manager now made sure that over a 3-week period he spoke to each employee on each shift at least once about something good he or she was doing.

After implementing these changes, the manager evaluated the results through continued tracking and comparison of these measures with the baseline data.

Evaluate. The illustration below shows the results of using recognition and encouragement to reinforce and strengthen good performance.

A definite improvement in productivity in the manager's department resulted from his intervention program. Although quantity of work completed dropped briefly at first, this measure then actually improved as well.

Source. Personal communication, line manager.

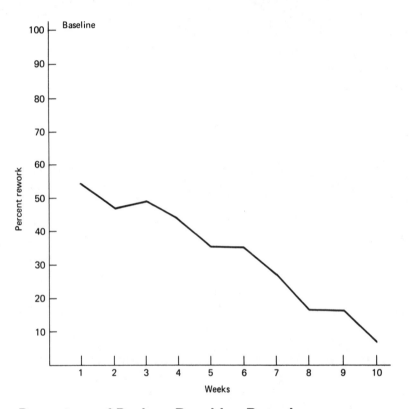

Percentage of Designs Requiring Rework

Case 13: Improving Safety Practices in Two Departments of a Wholesale Bakery

---

Pinpoint. Improving performance on a list of safety items.

Track. A list of safety items was compiled for each of the departments and data were collected on the percentage of those items performed safely by each department as a whole. These data showed that the make-up department was averaging 70 percent and the wrapping department 77.6 percent.

Analyze. Research indicates that the overwhelming number of on-the-job accidents can be attributed to unsafe acts on the part of workers, rather than to unsafe mechanical or physical working conditions. A behavioral analysis of conditions at the bakery revealed that safe practices were probably not being maintained because there was little, if any, positive reinforcement for performing safely, and when employees did perform unsafely, they rarely (relative to the number of unsafe acts) experienced an injury.

Change. To make sure the employees knew what constituted good safety practices, a 30-minute safety information session was held. A departmental goal of 90 percent safe performance was then established, and reinforcement was provided in the form of feedback to each department on the percentage of items they performed safely as a group. This information was entered on a graph and posted in the work area. In addition, each supervisor was requested to recognize workers when he saw them performing safely. In turn, the president and the plant manager were asked to follow through and check at least once weekly with the supervisors on the progress of the safety program.

Evaluate. The visual feedback provided by the graph and the verbal feedback provided by the supervisory personnel resulted in the following improvements in safety performance: an increase for the Make-up department from an average of 70 percent to an average of 95.8 percent, and from 77.6 percent in the Wrapping department to 99.3 percent. Again, it was simply a matter of building on good performance and letting people know their efforts had been noticed.

Reference. Komaki, J., Barwick, K. D., and Scott, L. R. A behavioral approach to occupational safety: Pinpointing and reinforcing safe performance in a food manufacturing plant. *Journal of Applied Psychology* 4:434–445, 1978.

Case 14: Use of a Recognition and Reinforcement Program to Improve Sales Behaviors at Mobil Oil in Bogota, Colombia

---

Pinpoint. Six specific behaviors of sales representatives were targeted for improvement: increasing frequency of sales calls; providing specified information on calls made; increasing frequency of calls on wholesale salesmen to train them in Mobil product information and sales techniques; providing information on those calls; using credit information correctly; and providing demographic data on new customers.

Track. Eleven sales representatives were involved in the project. Each of the six pinpointed behaviors was tracked for each of the eleven representatives.

Analyze. A behavioral analysis showed the need for improved feedback to the sales representatives on how effectively they were performing the six target behaviors.

Change. The feedback system implemented at the site involved graphing the performance of the salesmen on a weekly basis and sending all the data back out to all eleven individuals so that their performance was made public. In addition, the salesmen would come in from Colombia once a month to a sales meeting, at which time every member of the sales department would publicly review his performance during the previous month. At the end of the meeting, cash awards were made to the salesmen separate from their regular paychecks.

Evaluate. The project consultant noted that the salesmen were initially quite anxious about their reports, but that as time went on, the sales meetings began to turn into something more closely akin to in-service training programs. The salesmen began to advise each other on solutions to problems in terms of what technique or procedure had worked for them.

In addition to the recognition and reinforcement program, Mobil introduced a number of policy changes at the Bogota site during this period. Collectively, these changes, including the recognition and reinforcement program, resulted in a 28 percent increase in sales.

Source. Personal communication, Carl Pitts Associates.

Case 15: Improving Customer Service in a Fast Food Franchise

Pinpoint. The president of a fast food chain expressed interest in improving the friendliness of front-line personnel. Following extensive discussions, two behaviors were identified to describe a friendly employee: smiling at and talking with customers.

Track. Direct observations were made by training observers to assess individual levels of friendliness. An observer acting as a customer sat in the dining area and recorded data for 15 minutes on a wallet-sized card while completing his or her meal. The observer noted whether the pinpointed behaviors occurred in the presence of a customer at two different areas within the store, the cash register and the dining area.

A behavior sampling method of tracking was used. Each observation was divided into 10-second intervals. Raters observed for 10 seconds and then recorded during the next 10 seconds. The observers recorded their observations by placing a check in the appropriate space on the data card if a customer was present and if any of the behaviors occurred. The percentage of time employees smiled and talked with customers in each area was then computed.

Observations were conducted five to seven times each week for a period of 13 weeks. To maximize the probability that customers would be present, almost all (85.9 percent) of the observations were made during the busiest time of the week.

Analyze. During the 3 weeks of establishing the baseline, a behavioral analysis, that is, an examination of the antecedents and consequences of performance, was conducted to determine what might be hindering employees from being more friendly. The formal training, which all employees received before working in the store, did include the service objective of encouraging customers to return. Suggestions were made during training about how to reach that objective (greeting customers, smiling sincerely, asking if it was the customer's first visit, giving a warm goodbye). Although training emphasized the importance of customer service, it appeared that the quality of customer service suffered because of a lack of consequences given on the job. The manager herself was an excellent model of friendliness, but she spent most of her time in food preparation and maintenance. She rarely recognized employees for acting in a friendly manner. An occasional reminder was given, but a single smile or conversation with a customer was usually the result, after which prompts would cease.

Change. Looking first at the cash register area, baseline data showed that talking with customers occurred at the high rate of 88.1 percent, while smiling occurred only 41.2 percent of the time. It was therefore decided to single out smiling for improvement. First, the store manager presented the idea of increasing friendliness to the employees. She pointed out the public nature of their jobs and the importance of learning how to interact with customers. Friendliness was behaviorally defined, with emphasis on smiling. It was suggested that each employee smile at least four times when taking an order from a customer at the cash register. Four cues for smiling at the cash register position were designated: when (1) greeting, (2) taking the order, (3) asking about the dessert special, and (4) giving the customer change. Capitalizing on the infectious nature of smiling, the store manager suggested that employees see whether customers smiled in return, thereby drawing their attention to a natural and immediate consequence of smiling. The second consequence was provided by employees themselves in the form of a self-recording checklist posted by the time clock. At the end of their shifts, employees estimated how often they smiled following the four cues and whether customers smiled back. The third consequence was provided by the manager in the form of praise and recognition. The manager was asked to comment at least once each day to each employee seen smiling at the cash register. The manager also filled out a checklist at the end of the day. Her checklist included items about her own behavior at the register, customers smiling back, and reminding and recognizing employees for friendliness.

In the dining area interventions were introduced after 6, 8, and 10 weeks, respectively. In this area, talking with customers (rather than smiling) was emphasized because it was noted that once employees approached a tableful of customers and initiated a brief conversation, they almost always smiled at customers.

Three different interventions were used. Intervention 1 was similar to the intervention for smiling at the cash register. In a training session the store manager pointed out that beginning conversations is a valuable social skill and that it is something that can be learned and improved with practice. She suggested some "opening lines," and encouraged employees to discuss topics of their own. Employees practiced starting and continuing conversations with the manager. Cues were identified: (1) when picking up a tray in the dining area, (2) when there were no customers in the cash register or packaging areas, and (3) after suggesting a dessert special. Three consequences were established. First, employees were encouraged to see how many customers they could get to speak with them. Second, the employee checklist was revised to include three items concerned with talking to customers in the dining room. Third, the store manager agreed to recognize employees when they performed the desired behaviors.

During intervention 2, the manager assigned tables for which employees would be responsible, and an informal contingency contract was set up in which employees earned a 5-minute break each hour for talking with at least five customers. Employees placed a check on a tablet placed behind the counter each time they initiated a conversation and each time the customer responded.

During intervention 3, employees approached customers in the dining area with a tent-shaped sign in hand. Employees were encouraged to use the subject of the signs as a topic of conversation. The signs described selected food items available in the restaurant. Following each conversation the employee left the "conversation tent" on the table. The manager agreed to make a graph of the percentage of customers who had been approached as defined by the number of occupied tables with conversation tents divided by the total number of occupied tables.

Evaluate. A total of 81 observations was collected over a 3-month period of time. In the cash register area, front-line personnel smiled less than half of the time (41.2 percent) during baseline. Following the intervention that focused on smiling, employees smiled on the average of two-thirds of the time (67.3 percent).

The results for talking and smiling in the dining area paralleled one another and were mixed. During intervention 1, there was no noticeable change in talking (baseline mean, 19.0 percent; intervention 1 mean, 16.6 percent). An analysis revealed that potentially reinforcing consequences were delayed and infrequent. Compared with returning a smile in the cash register area, customers in the dining area were less likely to speak in return. The manager also reported that she was less likely to recognize employees for talking with customers in the dining room. One reason was that the behaviors occurred less frequently. In the dining area employees talked and smiled with customers less than 20 percent of the time. However, employees engaged in these behaviors over 90 percent (talking) and 65 percent (smiling) of the time in the cash register area. Another reason was that it was difficult for the manager to determine accurately and quickly whether the behaviors had occurred. The behaviors occurred in less easily observed sections of the restaurant and left no tangible outcomes.

During intervention 2, in which employees provided their own consequences, talking with customers in the dining area doubled from baseline and intervention 1 means of 19 percent and 16.6 percent, respectively, to 35.1 percent. Unfortunately, however, problems arose in the implementation of intervention 2. Employees who were primarily responsible for cash register interactions complained because they did not have an opportunity to earn a break. Assigning employees tables for which each was responsible eliminated the problem of duplication; however, continual monitoring was necessary to ensure that all tables were covered at all times because of the complex scheduling of employees.

During intervention 3, talking with customers in the dining area returned to baseline levels (16 percent). The intervention, although promising, was not implemented as planned. Over half of the time the manager was out of town in preparation for a new job assignment. As a result, she rarely recognized employees or provided feedback in the form of a graph of their performance. Providing a topic of conversation for employees was not sufficient to maintain performance.

This study introduces an important but complicated behavioral arena to researchers. Perhaps its greatest contribution is to point out some of the problems encountered in measuring and improving customer service in a retail setting. It certainly also suggests the challenges to the ingenuity and persistence of researchers to be found in the area of customer service.

Reference. Komaki, J., Blood, M. R., and Holder, D. Fostering friendliness in a fast food franchise. *Journal of Organizational Behavior Management* 2:151–164, 1980.

Case 16: Use of a "Feedback Package" System, Designed to Prevent Occupational Accidents and to Fit Directly into the Normal Operations of an Industrial Organization

---

Pinpoint. The study was conducted in the main factory of a private industrial organization, which was divided into six major production departments.

Using Occupational Safety and Health Act terminology and hazard classifications, and with the assistance of several members of the company's Safety Committee, a list of possible hazardous conditions was developed. Six major categories included (1) obstructions of walking/ working surfaces; (2) exit, ladder, or sprinkler obstruction; (3) hazardous materials; (4) hazardous materials storage; (5) hazardous machine guarding; and (6) electrical hazards. These categories were subdivided into eighteen specific hazardous conditions to permit precise feedback.

Track. Data were recorded daily for 12 weeks at randomly chosen times. Observations took place during the first shift while the plant was in full operation, each session lasting from 15 to 20 minutes. All of the plant's production supervisors were aware that such information was being collected. The observer walked through each department, noting hazards, but did not record them until the end of each aisle was reached. (This procedure was designed to prevent the workers from noticing exactly what was being recorded.) The location of each hazard and its frequency of occurrence was then recorded on a map of the department's layout. Baselines were recorded for all six departments for three weeks.

Analyze. The main role of the plant's Safety Committee was to conduct unannounced monthly inspections to identify existing hazardous conditions in each department. After inspections, a written memo notified each department's supervisor of the identified hazards. Because this procedure had not reduced safety hazards to an acceptable level, more detailed feedback, along with verbal reinforcement for good practices, was substituted for the monthly inspections and memos from the Safety Committee.

Change. Following the 3 weeks of baseline feedback was first introduced with Departments 1 and 2, while baseline conditions were continued with the other four departments for the next 6 weeks. This sequence was then replicated with Departments 4 and 5, and after 9 weeks with Departments 3 and 6. The supervisors were requested not to communicate to others about the feedback program.

The change procedure consisted of a three-component "package": (1) feedback as to number and location of hazards, (2) specific suggestions for improvement, and (3) any positive evaluative comments merited by accomplishments. It took an average of 7 minutes to prepare each form. Written feedback was provided on company paper at a short meeting held with the production and/or personnel manager and the respective supervisor. The feedback was discussed and progress was emphasized. Threat or punishment was *never* used. Because management felt that a semiweekly schedule could be maintained following termination of the formal study, it was decided to provide the feedback twice a week. To ensure that supervisors understood the system, individual meetings were held with each of them prior to implementing the feedback package in their departments.

Evaluate. Overall, results were similar for all departments. During baseline, the mean frequency of hazards in Departments 1 and 2 was 30.1 and 28.8, respectively. This decreased to 13.2 and 5.7, respectively, during the change phase, whereas hazards among the other two groups remained approximately at baseline levels. The mean frequency of hazards for Departments 4 and 5 was 13.2 and 14.8 during baseline, decreasing to 8.4 and 1.8, respectively, during the feedback-suggestion phase. Departments 3 and 6 decreased from a baseline level of 38.6 and 14 to 12.9 and 9.9, respectively, during the change condition.

The primary value of the program was its simplicity and the ease with which it could be incorporated within a supervisor's routine. Once hazards were identified and defined (the major effort required by the program), inspections were carried out in about 10 to 15 minutes and it took only a few minutes to fill in each form. The same forms were used for observations and feedback, and no extensive training or expertise was required of plant safety inspectors. A long-range follow-up 4 months after the completion of the experimental intervention phase of this study indicated a highly favorable maintenance effect.

Reference. Sulzer-Azaroff, B., and de Santamaria, Consuelo M. Industrial safety hazard reduction through performance feedback. *Journal of Applied Behavior Analysis* 13:287–295, 1980.

Case 17: Reducing Elevator Energy Use: A Comparison of Posted Feedback and Reduced Elevator Convenience

Pinpoint. Elevators are often installed in small buildings to provide an alternative to stairs for handicapped users as well as to assist in the transportation of freight. However, these elevators are often used by individuals who could as easily use the stairs. Unnecessary elevator use can consume large amounts of energy and can deprive an individual of the opportunity to engage in a form of routine exercise (using the stairs). The purpose of this study was to compare the effects of two change procedures on the amount of energy consumed by three elevators located in two buildings of a small Canadian university.

Track. Energy consumption was measured by means of individual watt-hour meters wired to the main switchbox of each elevator. Meters on all three elevators were read between 1:00 and 1:15 p.m. Monday through Friday. Energy consumption was not measured on weekends or holidays because few people used the university buildings on these days. Therefore, only four data points were collected each week. These points represented the difference between the readings of each two consecutive days, that is, Monday and Tuesday, Tuesday and Wednesday, and so on. Baseline measures were taken for 1 week.

Analyze. Previous research in this area had utilized three basic strategies, either in isolation or together, to reduce unnecessary energy consumption. These were prompts, feedback, and incentives. Although incentives have produced large reductions in energy use, their use has not been cost effective in most cases. The effects of feedback and prompts have been equivocal. This study utilized prompts and feedback as one change procedure, and increasing the time required to travel between floors as another.

Change. During the feedback phase, white posterboard signs were mounted directly above the elevator call buttons located on each floor. Printed on the signs was the message: "Electricity consumed by users of this elevator: Last week___kw-hr. Best record___kw-hr." Numbers announcing weekly consumption were printed on white index cards using a black felt-tipped pen, and were affixed to the signs using clear plastic tape. Numbers were changed every Monday at 1:30 p.m. and represented the difference between the meter readings at 1:00 p.m. on that day and the meter reading at 1:00 p.m. on the preceding Monday.

Numbers announcing "best record" consumption were constructed and affixed to the sign in the same manner. However, best record numbers were printed using a red felt-tipped pen and were changed only when the previous week's total consumption was lower than the previous best record.

During the feedback-plus-prompts phase, the posted feedback on energy use continued as before. In addition, three different posters requesting people to use the stairs were mounted on each elevator door at each floor.

Next came a second baseline phase. Finally the delay in operation of the elevator doors was introduced, which increased the time required to travel between floors. During the door-delay phase, a delay of 16 seconds was added to the elevator door-closing mechanism, so that instead of 10 seconds it now took 26 seconds to close. In the final phase, the door delay was reduced from 26 to 21 seconds.

All phases of the study following the first baseline were introduced in a staggered fashion across the two buildings in which the elevators were located.

Evaluate. Energy consumption by all three elevators remained at baseline levels during the feedback and the feedback-plus-posters conditions. Delaying door closure, however, reduced energy consumption immediately and substantially in all three elevators (31 percent, 29 percent, and 33 percent). Reduction of the door delay from 26 to 21 seconds did not result in increased energy consumption by any of the elevators.

An alternative interpretation might suggest that the delayed door closure conserved electricity through mechanical rather than behavioral means. Increasing the door delay automatically decreased the amount of time that was available for the elevator to travel from floor to floor. Thus, the imposition of a long door delay may have made it physically impossible for the elevators to make as many trips as they had during baseline. A follow-up experiment, however, confirmed the results of the first study by demonstrating that energy was saved as a result of a change in behavior and not merely through mechanical means.

Reference.   Van Houten, R., Nau, P. A., and Merrigan, M. Reducing elevator energy use: A comparison of posted feedback and reduced elevator convenience. *Journal of Applied Behavior Analysis* 14:377–387, 1981.

APPENDIX TWO
BOOKS AND ARTICLES FOR FURTHER READING

Adam, E. E., Jr. Behavior modification in quality control. *Academy of Management Journal*, 18:662–679, 1975.

At Emery Air Freight: Positive reinforcement boosts performance. *Organizational Dynamics*, 1(3):41–50, 1973.

Beatty, R., and Schneier, C. E. Training the hard core unemployed through positive reinforcement. *Human Resource Management*, pp. 11–17, Winter 1972.

Beecroft, Jay L. How behavior modification improves productivity at 3M. *Training HRD*, pp. 83–95, October 1976.

Bobele, H. K., and Buchanan, P. Behavior modification: A tool for getting things done. *The Business Quarterly*, pp. 37–41, Winter 1975.

Brown, P. L. Management by Consequences. *Education & Training*, p. 286, October, 1981.

Brown, P. L., and Casley, M. Behavior modification: Getting down to business. *NPSI Journal*, p. 3, March 1979.

Brown, P. L., and Presbie, R. J. *Behavior Modification in Business, Industry and Government*. Champaign, Ill.: Research Press, 1976.

Connellan, Thomas K. *How to Improve Human Performance: Behaviorism in Business and Industry*. New York: Harper & Row, 1978.

Contingency management in a bank branch office. *Behavior Improvement News*, 2(10):2, 1978.

Dick, H. W. Increasing the productivity of the day relief textile machine operator. *Journal of Organizational Behavior Management*, 2(1):45–57, 1978.

Galego Oil: Incentives and training increase productivity. *Fuel Oil and Heat*, 35(12):27–28, 1976.

Gilbert, Thomas F. *Human Competence: Engineering Worthy Performance*. New York: McGraw-Hill, 1978.

Gupton, T., and LeBow, M. D. Behavior management in a large industrial firm. *Behavior Therapy*, 2:78–82, 1971.

Hamner, W. C., and Hamner, E. P. Behavior modification and the bottom line. *Organizational Dynamics*, pp. 12–14, Spring 1976.

Hermann, J. A., deMontes, A. I., Dominguez, B., Montes, F., and Hopkins, B. L. Effects of bonuses for punctuality on the tardiness of industrial workers. *Journal of Applied Behavior Analysis*, 6:563–570, 1973.

Kempen, R., and Hall, R. Vance. Reduction of industrial absenteeism: Results of a behavioral approach. *Journal of Organizational Behavior Management*, 1(1):1–21, 1977.

Komaki, J., Barwick, K. D., and Scott, L. R. A behavioral approach to occupational safety: Pinpointing and reinforcing safe performance in a food manufacturing plant. *Journal of Applied Psychology*, in press.

Komaki, J., Waddel, W. M., and Pearce, M. G. The applied behavior analysis approach and individual employees: Improving performance in two small businesses. *Organizational Behavior and Human Performance*, 19:337–352, 1977.

Luthans, F., and Kreitner, P. *Organizational Behavior Modification.* Glenview, Ill.: Scott Foresman, 1975.

Miller, L. M. *Behavior Management: The New Science of Managing People at Work.* New York: John Wiley, 1978.

Pedalino, E., and Gamboa, V. W. Behavior modification and absenteeism: Intervention in one industrial setting. *Journal of Applied Psychology*, 59:694–698, 1974.

Performance management pays off for 3M Canada. *Training HRD*, pp. 36–46, January 1979.

Productivity gains from a pat on the back. *Business Week*, pp. 56–58, Jan. 23, 1978.

Reinforcement: Its effect on paint sales. *Behavior Improvement News*, 3(1):4, 1979.

Rout, L. Office output: White collar workers start to get attention in productivity studies. *The Wall Street Journal*, 194(26):1, Aug. 7, 1979.

Warren, M. W. Using behavioral technology to improve sales performance. *Training and Development Journal*, pp. 54–56, July 1978.

Where Skinner's theories work. *Business Week*, pp. 64–65, Dec. 2, 1972.

Zemke, Ron. Behavioral observations: Why the "count and chart" approach to task analysis pays off. *Training HRD*, pp. 90–93, September 1979.

APPENDIX THREE
SAMPLE WORKSHEETS

The illustration on page 172 is an overview of the MBC Decision-Making Process. The sample worksheets that follow, starting on page 173, are designed for your use. Permission is granted to reproduce single copies; if multiple copies are required, please write to Instructional Design Associates, P. O. Box 296, New Paltz, New York 12561.

The MBC Decision-Making Process

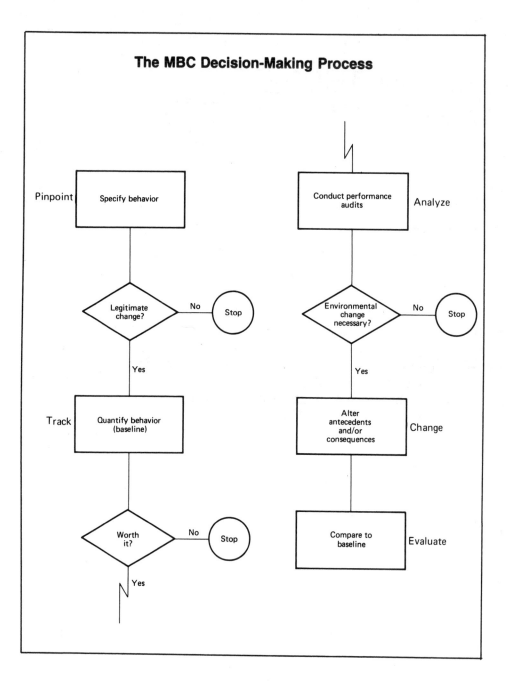

172

Pinpointing Form

DESIRABLE	UNDESIRABLE
Employee(s)	Employee(s)
Peer(s)	Peer(s)
Manager(s)	Manager(s)
Significant other(s)	Significant other(s)

Tracking Form

1. Write the pinpointed behavior of concern in Column 1.
2. Specify the tracking method in Column 2.
3. Specify *what* will be tracked, along with *where* and *when* the tracking will take place, in Column 3.

    1. Behavior—continuous tracking (all)
    2. Behavior sampling (some)
    3. Product—continuous tracking (all)
    4. Product sampling (some)

1. Pinpointed behavior	2. Tracking method	3. (a) What, (b) Where, (c) When
	3	

An A-B-C Analysis Form

Instructions:
1. Transfer the pinpointed behaviors of concern from the Pinpointing form to the Behavior column (column 2).
2. In column 1, list as many antecedents as you can think of for each behavior.
3. In column 3, list as many consequences as you can think of for each behavior.
4. In column 4, indicate the "probable effect" of each consequence.

Antecedent(s)	Behavior	Consequence(s)	Probable Effect (Reinforcement- Punishment- None)
1.			
2.			
3.			
4.			

A Balance of Consequences Audit Form

DESIRED BEHAVIOR: _____

1.	2.
Reinforcing consequences	Punishing consequences

UNDESIRED BEHAVIOR: _____

3.	4.
Reinforcing consequences	Punishing consequences

IMPACT	TIMELINESS	PROBABILITY
Personal or Other	Immediate or Delayed	Certain or Uncertain

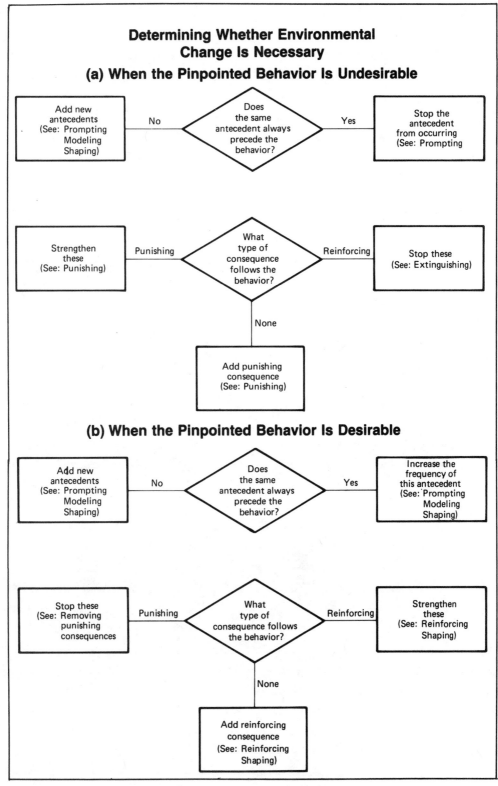

Determining Whether Environmental Change Is Necessary

(a) When the Pinpointed Behavior Is Undesirable

| Add new antecedents (See: Prompting Modeling Shaping) | ← No — | Does the same antecedent always precede the behavior? | — Yes → | Stop the antecedent from occurring (See: Prompting |

| Strengthen these (See: Punishing) | ← Punishing — | What type of consequence follows the behavior? | — Reinforcing → | Stop these (See: Extinguishing) |

None

Add punishing consequence (See: Punishing)

(b) When the Pinpointed Behavior Is Desirable

| Add new antecedents (See: Prompting Modeling Shaping) | ← No — | Does the same antecedent always precede the behavior? | — Yes → | Increase the frequency of this antecedent (See: Prompting Modeling Shaping) |

| Stop these (See: Removing punishing consequences | ← Punishing — | What type of consequence follows the behavior? | — Reinforcing → | Strengthen these (See: Reinforcing Shaping) |

None

Add reinforcing consequence (See: Reinforcing Shaping)

Performance Improvement
Work Action Plan

_____   _____
           Name   Position

1. Pinpoint
   Behavior _____
   _____
   _____
   Where exhibited _____
   How performance related _____
   (output measure?)

2. Track
   How counted _____
   Where counted _____
   When and for how long _____

3. Analyze (see A-B-C Analysis and/or B-O-C Audit)

4. Change
   Indicate your proposed intervention strategy. (This will include changes
   in either antecedents, consequences, or both.)
   _____
   _____
   _____
   _____
   _____
   Starting date _____
   Duration _____

5. Evaluate
   Description of amount of change which will be deemed satisfactory
   (standards or goals)
   _____
   _____
   _____
   Cost-effectiveness measures (economic payoffs) _____

INDEX